Sharing Your Faith

Selwyn Hughes

Marshalls

Other books and booklets by Selwyn Hughes

Discovering Your Place in the Body of Christ
Fifteen Ways to a More Effective Prayer Life
Now You Are a Christian
Seven Steps to Overcoming Depression
Ten Principles for a Happy Marriage

Marshall Paperbacks
Marshall Morgan & Scott

3 Beggarwood Lane, Basingstoke, Hants RG23 7LP

Copyright © Selwyn Hughes 1983
First published by Marshall Morgan & Scott 1983
Reprinted
Impression No:
  84 85 86–10 9 8 7 6 5 4 3

ISBN 0 551 01043 6

Phototypeset by Input Typesetting Ltd., London
Printed in Great Britain by Richard Clay, Suffolk

Contents

Introduction

The last thing we need in the contemporary Christian Church is someone taking Christians to task over their individual responsibility to share the faith. So much has been said on this subject in the past, and some of it so strongly, that many Christians carry a heavy load of guilt as they compare their own Christian witness to that of the Early Church and the first disciples.

As a firsthand observer of the Christian scene for close on forty years, I am convinced that the Church is filled with casualties, who, having set out to share their faith and failed, sit back and defend their feelings of inadequacy by such statements as these: 'I'm not cut out for witnessing.' Or, 'My life is a witness – I can add nothing with my lips.' Or, 'I'm an introvert – introverts never make good witnesses.'

My purpose in writing this book is neither to add to the weight of guilt which many Christians feel over the issue of Christian witnessing, nor to provide them with excuses to enable them to get off the hook. Indeed, it is incumbent upon every Christian, at appropriate moments and in the right circumstances, to share the reality of Christ with his non-Christian friends and acquaintances. However, a balance is needed between evangelistic responsibility and the genuine difficulties which confront each one of us as we attempt to verbally present Christ to the world.

The main thesis of this book is that everyone can

present a positive witness to Jesus Christ – even introverts. Where most Christians go wrong is when they try to copy someone else rather than being themselves.

Witnessing, if it is to be successful, must be in harmony with one's basic temperament and personality, otherwise it comes across to non-Christians as phony and artificial. The only witnessing that is productive is natural witnessing – witnessing consistent with *who* and *what* you are.

If this book helps you to find the proper balance between your responsibility to witness and the person you are, then I will be more than amply rewarded. My concern is that you will be helped to share your faith, not as a mere duty – but as a delight.

Selwyn Hughes
March 1983

1: Good News is for telling

The world is waiting for good news. Men and women anxiously scan the headlines of the morning papers, searching for some glimmer of hope in the slow, dark depressing development of international politics. They are gripped by a gloom and a despondency such as no generation has experienced since the beginning of recorded time.

What has brought about this modern mood of cynicism and despair? An awareness that:

Millions starve . . . and need not.

Racial hatred threatens to erupt in bloody battles on our streets.

Ideological antagonisms swell and fester, threatening to burst at any moment.

Human life is cheap – as evidenced by the millions of aborted babies each year.

Politicians and economists struggle to hold the economy together, but seem to be fighting a losing battle.

Family life is breaking apart, and we are told that by the beginning of the 21st century, the family unit, as we now know it, may no longer exist.

Then, of course, there is the bomb!

We dwell in the darkness of nuclear night. It is

foolish to deny it. All thinking men and women know that human slaughter can now be achieved on a scale only dreamed about by ancient conquerors.

I watched the television series produced by Carl Sagan entitled *Cosmos*, and a phrase he used still haunts me. 'In this generation,' he said, 'the world's entire population can be totally annihilated, not in a month, a week, or even in a day . . . but in the length of a lazy afternoon.'

Of course, people are uniting all over the world to say: 'It must not be.' But no matter what agreements are made or what pacts are signed, the awful possibility still exists. Cynicism and despair eat into the hearts of ordinary men and women. They may not use the words, but the language of their fear-filled hearts is borrowed from the old paganism, 'Let us eat, drink and be merry, for tomorrow we die.'

Most thinking is taking place today against that sombre background, and any thought which completely ignores the issue is not in touch with life or reality. The pall of the nuclear bomb over-shadows the classroom, the home, the factory, the office, the shop and every avenue of life. It is not surprising, therefore, that the men and women of this generation, to whom the idea of some catastrophic end to the world was at one time a joke, are considering the idea in all seriousness. It is not surprising either that they react to this possibility with cynicism and despair.

The Good News

What, in the light of the world's ills, is the most important message mankind can be given?

Is there any doubt?

It is the Good News of the Gospel. It is news of God. This news: God has visited us in the person of His Son, Jesus Christ, to give new life to everyone who will receive it. The Living Bible puts it so well: 'When we were utterly helpless with no way of escape, Christ came at just the right time and died for us sinners who had no use for him' (Rom. 5:6).

The entire chapter explains and expounds in wonderful detail God's great plan of salvation. Take this, for example: 'Even if we were good, we really wouldn't expect anyone to die for us, though, of course, that might be barely possible. But God showed his great love for us by sending Christ to die for us while we were still sinners' (Rom. 5:7–8, TLB).

That's the wonder of the Gospel – that God, through His love, entered human history and made it possible for sinners to be forgiven and reconciled to a holy God. The Bible tells us that by faith – itself a gift of God – any poor bankrupt sinner can be united to the life of God. Once this happens, he can say with the apostle Paul: 'To me to live is Christ' (Phil. 1:21).

One of the greatest aspects of the Good News which Christ came to bring is its offer of *life*. Jesus said, 'I am come that they might have life, and that they might have it more abundantly' (John 10:10).

The life that Christ promises to give to any

9

stained and stunted sinner is not a higher degree of natural life, but a life that is completely different – the very life of God Himself.

A person can, as Dr W. E. Sangster once put it, 'have the life of God as *his* life . . . not just the *power* of Christ, or the *help* of Christ, or even *Christ-likeness*, but Christ Himself. The Saviour does not just save a sinner from without, but actually lives within; and thinks, feels and wills in the life of His consenting servant.'

Independent of circumstances

And this life does not depend on circumstances. No matter how dark or dismal the surroundings, in the heart of the person who has experienced a personal encounter with Christ, throbs a power that lifts him above his environment.

In the first century, when the Christian faith began to spread with all the rapidity of a prairie fire, the Romans, who were then the masters, fearing some secret disloyalty to Rome, persecuted the people who professed the faith and cast them to the lions. But those, in one sense, were the fortunate ones.

Louis Bertrand tells in one of his books of a harder, bitterer and more terrible sentence passed on those first-century Christians. It was called *damnatus ad metalla* – condemned to the mines. The sufferings they endured there were beyond description.

Under the lash of their Roman guards, they were forced to row their own galley to North Africa, and then began a trek across sun-baked territory to the Numidian mines.

Before being driven underground, they had their chains shortened, so that they could never stand upright again, and were branded on their foreheads with red hot irons. Then, with a lamp and a hammer, they were sent into the mines – never to return.

How did those early Christians react to such torment and torture? Bertrand says: 'Many of them wrote messages with charcoal on the smooth rock; prayers some of them, and the dear names of departed friends.' But those who visited the mines years later came across one word that was written over and over again. One historian said that it ran in long black lines 'like a flight of swallows chasing one another towards the light': *Vita, Vita, Vita*. Life, Life, Life.

Life? The early Christians had it. Whether it was facing the lions or incarcerated in the Numidian mines, they possessed a life that helped them rise above all their circumstances.

And this is the message we have to offer a confused and bewildered generation. By faith – itself a gift of God – sinners may be united to the life of God. Their old self may die and they may say with the apostle Paul, 'For to me to live is Christ' (Phil. 1:21).

It is incredible – but true.

Only effective if accepted

However, the fact that God has provided a wonderful offer of salvation for us is, in itself, inadequate. Man is still lost until he accepts that salvation and receives it as a gift.

In this broad-minded age we hardly ever hear

the condition of non-Christians being described as 'lost'. But that is precisely their condition apart from Jesus Christ.

One evangelist says, 'The conviction that men and women are lost outside of Jesus Christ suffers from tired blood.' Many believers are embarrassed to refer to the unconverted as 'lost', but this is exactly how the Bible describes their condition.

Michael Green says, 'If you believe that outside of Christ there is no hope, it is impossible to possess an atom of human love and kindness without being gripped with the great desire to bring men to this one way of salvation.' It was this conviction that fired the Early Church and made them such earnest soul-winners. They reasoned thus: if man is made for God . . . and if he can be saved or lost eternally . . . then the most important thing in the world is to show men and women how they can be saved.

Why is it that many modern-day Christians fail to recognise that humanity (according to the Scriptures) is divided into categories of saved and lost? Leighton Ford thinks it is because we Christians have imbibed the spirit of the age – tolerance. He says, 'We worship at the shrine of the great god *Tolerance*. The modern mind has shifted into neutral, disliking the pain of distinguishing right from wrong, the truth from falsehood. Freedom has come to mean that each person is responsible for himself and no one should try to change another.'

If we find it difficult to develop a mind-set that sees people as saved or lost, then it is time we opened up our Bibles. Jesus, in the Gospels, talked about travelling one of two roads, serving one of two masters, and choosing between one of two destinies. Let there be no misunderstanding on the issue – man is *lost*, eternally and irretrievably lost unless he repents of his sin and receives into his life the benefits of Christ's atonement.

No place to hide

The greatest tragedy of our time is the fact that man, in his lost condition, is attempting to hide away from God, while God, in His love, attempts to tell him that a way has been made by which he can have his sin forgiven and be restored to God's favour.

One of the first things Adam and Eve did after they ate of the forbidden fruit was to run and hide from God among the trees of the Garden. And man has been trying to hide from God ever since.

Just recently the newspapers carried the story of a middle-aged man, Norman Green, who was a fugitive from the police. Norman had spent eight years living in a 'tomb' under the floorboards of his home because he thought he was a suspect in a police investigation over the mysterious death of an eighty-seven year old woman.

Despite his innocence, when the police first questioned Norman about the death of the old woman, he became desperately afraid. Thinking that he would be separated from his family, he hollowed out a small space under the floorboards of his home where he concealed himself.

When the police investigation had been completed, they attempted to interview Norman to let him know that he had been eliminated from their enquiries, but they were told by his wife,

Pauline, that he had left both her and the children, and his whereabouts were not known.

The truth was that, by day, Pauline acted the role of a lonely divorcee, struggling to bring up six children on her own, but, by night, she provided a lifeline for her husband by handing food and drink down to him in the twenty-one inch hole beneath the lounge floor, where he lay in total darkness.

When finally the story came out, and Norman learned he had nothing to fear, he said, 'It's amazing how I stuck it so long. It's strange how one can adjust to living like that.'

What a waste of eight years. Here was Norman doing his best to avoid the police, thinking they wanted to accuse him, while all the time they were doing their best to find him to let him know that he had nothing to fear.

Norman is representative of every man and woman who hides from God. They fear the Almighty because they think He wants to condemn them, while in fact the reverse is true. God is eager to meet with sinners to tell them that by virtue of Christ's sacrifice on Calvary they have nothing to fear. The Bible says that Christ has come not to condemn the world but to save it. When Jesus uttered those matchless words in John 3:16: 'For God loved the world so much that he gave his only Son,' he went on to say: 'God did not send his Son into the world to condemn it, but to save it' (John 3:17, TLB). No wonder such a message is called the *Gospel* or Good News!

We are Christ's ambassadors

But how is such Good News to be made known?

Through the lips and lives of those who have experienced Christ's transforming power. In other words – if you are a committed Christian – *through you and me*.

The apostle Paul, when emphasising the responsibility of all Christians to tell others the Good News of the Gospel, said, 'We are Christ's ambassadors. God is using us to speak to you: we beg you, as though Christ himself were here pleading with you, receive the love he offers you – be reconciled to God' (2 Cor. 5:20, TLB). The obligation to be an ambassador of Jesus Christ is laid on all Christians. To belong to Him and yet not represent Him before the world is criminal.

I remember, many years ago, hearing a great British preacher expound on the text to which I have just referred.

'Everyone knows,' he said, 'that an ambassador is one who represents his own country in an alien land. If that country is a monarchy, the ambassador is regarded as the personal representative of the king (or queen), and it is expected that he will be accredited the honours and distinctions which belong, not to him as a person, but to the one in whose place he stands.'

An ambassador's allegiance is to his own land and to his own king. He dwells as an Englishman (or an American) in another country, but he is not of it. His citizenship and his loyalty are all elsewhere.

It is a high office. And you – if you are a

committed servant of the Lord Jesus Christ – are an ambassador.

Just after the last war, an intriguing book appeared in Britain entitled *Ambassador on Special Mission*. It was written by Lord Templewood, better known as Sir Samuel Hoare. It told the story of his dispatch to Spain at a most critical period during the Second World War. His instructions were to keep Franco out of the struggle, for at that time England was at an extremely difficult phase. Franco was known to be pro-Nazi and pro-fascist. Lord Templewood understood the Spanish mind so well, and presented his case so effectively to Franco, that he never came into the war against us. Lord Templewood had the credit for that. Historians say that it might have complicated our position at that time had Spain come into the war against us, but Lord Templewood performed his ambassadorial duties well.

We, too, are ambassadors on special mission! Remember how Paul put it? 'We beg you, as though Christ himself were here pleading with you, receive the love he offers you – be reconciled to God.'

God is saying to this generation, as He did to Israel of old: 'As I live, says the Lord God, I have no pleasure in the death of the wicked; *I desire that the wicked turn from his evil ways and live*. Turn, turn from your wickedness, for why will you die, O Israel?' (Ezek. 33:11, TLB).

Why will you die? That is the message God wants us to convey to the men and women of our age. This is the heart of the evangel; this is the core of the Gospel. Christ died on the cross so that we do not have to die. Christ also suffered.

He died once for the sins of all us guilty sinners . . . 'that he might bring us safely home to God' (1 Peter 3:18, TLB). 'He is not willing that any should perish, and he is giving more time for sinners to repent' (2 Peter 3:9, TLB).

As Christ's ambassadors, we are to face the world and say, in effect; 'I am from God, I am an ambassador of the King of kings. I have been commissioned by Him to tell you that He wants to be reconciled to you. Though you have deeply offended Him and have broken His laws, He loves you so much that He has taken the initiative and died on a cross so that you might be eternally pardoned. Accept the pardon He bestows, and you can be reconciled to God.'

You would not use those precise words (people would think you mad!), but that should be the tenor of your message. Our 'special mission' is to reconcile men and women to a holy God. What a task! Oh the privilege and wonder of being able to say to the vilest sinner – 'My God wants to be reconciled to you!'

Do we have a right to 'interfere'?

But what do we say to those who claim that our passion to share the Good News with the world is 'interference in a person's human rights'? There is an increasing multitude of people who believe that. They *pride* themselves on believing it. They think they are advanced, broad-minded and enlightened to entertain those views. Sharing the faith, by implication, is the occupation of bigots.

Let me answer it in this way. Suppose someone

suffered a deep cut, say, on their forearm. What is the best way to treat it?

In some parts of the world there are those who would say it should be covered with cow dung. Elsewhere there are those who would say one should carry a lucky charm which will help to make one well very soon.

Most people, however, believe that the best way to treat a wound is to wash it clean and apply some antiseptic to it.

Whatever views people might have we *know* that the last of the methods I have described above is the best.

It is the same with the faith we are called upon to proclaim. Just as the world has the right to know that the *best* way to treat a wound is by cleaning it and applying antiseptic to it, so does it have a right to know that the way to obtain eternal life and joy is through a personal encounter with Jesus Christ. It is not 'interfering in a person's human rights' to do that; it is plain humanity to do so.

Just suppose that some Russian scientists discovered a cure for cancer. And suppose, after having done so, they decided to keep it a close secret and apply treatment only to members of the 'iron curtain' countries. That would be a crime against the whole of humanity. The same indictment would apply if such a cure were found in any country of the world, and its leaders or scientists failed to make it known. If we, to whom it had pleased God to reveal Himself in Jesus Christ, were to keep the knowledge of His offer of eternal salvation to ourselves, then it would be a crime against the whole of the human race.

Jesus said, 'You will receive power when the Holy Spirit comes on you; and you will be my witnesses' (Acts 1:8, NIV). That one statement alone, apart from the scores of other commands in Scripture, would be enough reason for sharing our faith with the world.

Our Saviour's command is reinforced by the unspeakable need of people who live in this nuclear age.

Frightened, dejected, devoid of hope, they are waiting for Good News.

This news: '. . . nothing can ever separate us from his love. Death can't, and life can't. The angels won't, and all the powers of hell itself cannot keep God's love away. Our fears for today, our worries about tomorrow, or where we are – high above the sky, or in the deepest ocean – nothing will ever be able to separate us from the love of God demonstrated by our Lord Jesus Christ when he died for us' (Rom. 8:38–39. TLB).

Our task is to proclaim it.

The only question is 'How?'

2: Why so much reluctance?

If Good News is for telling why are Christians so reluctant to tell it? When one thinks of the zeal of convinced Leftists or the burning enthusiasm of social reformers, running around with their latest nostrum for the world's ills, how strange it is that so many Christians can be so tepid over the vital task of sharing Christ's love with a lost world.

There are notable exceptions, of course, but, generally speaking, when it comes to the matter of sharing the faith far too many of us are like the Arctic rivers – frozen at the mouth!

I'll never forget hearing Charles Potter speak at a Youth for Christ Rally many years ago in Torquay, Devon. Charles was an ex-Communist who found Christ. He said that when he became a Communist he was impressed, not only with the basic principles of Communism, but with the zeal and enthusiasm of each of its members.

'I was staggered,' he said, 'by the commitment of my friends who would go without sleep or get up early in the morning to stand outside a factory gate and distribute Communist literature. Time and time again, whenever I felt like a lie-in, I would remind myself of those who, prior to going to their own jobs, would give up an hour to stand in all kinds of weather, giving out leaflets that communicated the Communist message.'

'But imagine my surprise,' he went on, 'when after becoming a Christian, and realising that I now had a message that was far more powerful and revolutionary than Communism could ever conceive, I found that the majority of Christians, while they drooled over it in church made little or no effort to share it in their daily contacts.'

Of course Charles was the first to admit that you can't employ Communist methods of propaganda when sharing the Christian faith. Things like aggressively thrusting leaflets into people's hands, or buttonholing them in the streets and pressing them into argument, are not the best ways of securing a person's interest and attention. But Charles could never understand why it was that Communists could be so enthusiastic and, in general, Christians so half-hearted and nonchalant.

He told me privately that he experienced continual sadness over the general indifference of most Christians toward the subject of personal evangelism. He has now gone to be with the Lord, and, as far as I know, he went to his grave carrying that feeling of sadness.

Why is it that when it comes to sharing the Good News we are so lethargic and indifferent? There are several reasons why Christians lack evangelistic zeal. Let's consider them one by one:

Wrong teaching and modelling

Some Christians are reluctant to share the faith because of *exposure to wrong teaching and wrong modelling*.

I was a victim of this in the early part of my Christian experience. An evangelist came to my church who was a forceful and powerful speaker. He won people to Christ, not only in the services, but out on the streets as well. Throughout the day he went from door to door in the village inviting people to the services, and he seemed to know exactly what to say to people in whatever situation he found them. I was a teenager at the time, and I accompanied him one day to the local colliery.

A group of men were about to go down into the mine when he confronted them with the question: 'Will your last trip be up or down?' They paused for a moment and listened to him outline the way of salvation. I know for a fact that one of the men was converted to Christ right there on the spot.

During the weeks that he conducted the crusade in our little village church, he challenged us to be bold and adventurous in sharing Christ. 'Follow the principles I use,' he said, 'and they will work for you just as they work for me.'

A few weeks after he had gone, I found myself at the top of a mine shaft watching the men go down into the mine, and just as the cage began to slowly disappear down the shaft, I plucked up my courage and shouted, 'Will your last trip be up or down?' I shall never forget the expression on the men's faces as they vanished from my sight. I heard one of them say, 'He must be a candidate for Abergavenny House!' (the local Mental Institution).

I tried to follow several other of the evangelist's methods, but none of them seemed to work. The result was that I soon became loaded down with guilt, and gave up altogether the task of witnessing for Jesus Christ. It wasn't until years later, when someone took me aside and said to me, 'You don't have to be an evangelist, just be a witness.' that the light dawned. The Acts of the Apostles says: 'You are to be my witnesses.' But the teachers and preachers who came to our church interpreted that to mean: 'You are to be my evangelists.'

My friend told me that there are certain people in the Body of Christ, the Church, who are specifically called to be evangelists. They are equipped by God for the purpose of bringing large numbers of people to Christ.

'Just be a witness,' said my friend, 'and if God wants you to be an evangelist, then He will develop your basic gifts and equip you for the task.' Wise words. At that moment, the guilt I felt, due to my inability to live up to the standards set for me by preachers and teachers in my church, immediately dissolved. I was free – free to be myself and to witness for Christ without strain.

Later, God called me to be an evangelist, and when His call came I found an inner reinforcement that enabled me to move beyond the small circle in which I worked to call large numbers of men and women to Christ. But how glad I am for the wise words of my friend that day. They enabled me to relax, be myself, and to graduate

23

effortlessly from one level to another in the plans and purposes of God.

The question might be asked: what is a witness?

A witness is a person whose speech, conduct and daily life testify to the truth of Christ's Gospel. We witness mainly by our lives, and, when appropriate, of course, by our lips. We must get away from the idea, however, that every person we talk to must be presented with a high-powered evangelistic spiel such as 'The Four Spiritual Laws' or the 'ABC of Salvation'. There will be times when such a presentation will be appropriate, but, generally speaking, witnessing is showing the non-Christian community, *by our attitudes to life*, that we have found Hope in a hopeless world.

Because of exposure to wrong teaching and wrong modelling, the cause of evangelism has been greatly hampered. I know many Christians who are so loaded down with guilt because they cannot share the Gospel as powerfully or as methodically as others, that they have given up all attempts to witness for Christ. Embarrassed and humiliated, they have withdrawn from anything to do with evangelism.

In my own experience, when I set about the task of quietly witnessing for Christ – with no gimmicks, no pseudo-questionnaires, no button-holing of people and asking them, 'Are you saved?' – I saw more of my friends won to Christ than I ever saw in the days when I was an evangelical mugger. When my witnessing was natural, it became doubly effective.

'The best argument for Christianity is Christians,' says Sheldon Vanauken, 'their joy, their certainty, their completeness.'

No deep experience of Christ

Another reason why we are reluctant to share the faith is because *we do not have a deep ongoing experience of Christ, and consequently we have nothing to give away.*

Many of us are deeply disturbed when confronted with our responsibility to say a good word for Jesus Christ, because it reveals the poverty of our own spiritual condition. Instinctively we feel we ought to be able to give ourselves in some way to the task of making Christ known, but the most we can say is this: 'Let me introduce you to our minister. He will help you find the Lord.'

Jesus Christ once told a woman: 'Whoever drinks the water I give him will never thirst. Indeed, the water I give him will become in him a spring of water welling up to everlasting life' (John 4:14, NIV).

However, such a word is not fulfilled in us. We stumble from one day to another, living perhaps on a Christian book we have read, or the faith of our more spiritually-minded friends. Our confidence is not based directly on God, but on things that are related to Him.

I can remember a time in my own experience when although I was a minister and preaching several times a week, my life was spiritually bankrupt and barren. I had no deep abiding sense of Christ's presence in my heart. I talked to others about Christ, but it was always a great effort, done largely from a sense of duty rather than delight. I tried to convey the freshness of the 'water of life' to others, but my own heart was like a rusty pipe. Oh, how dull and dreary were those few months.

Then one night God, in His great love, revealed Himself to me in such a way that I fell upon my knees in an attitude of repentance. I had allowed myself to become so familiar with spiritual truth that it bred indifference. I had become a purveyor of doctrine rather than a herald of the King. The responsibility for my indifference was mine and mine alone. I could blame no one but myself. And when I asked God's forgiveness for my lack of zeal, the shackles that were binding my spirit fell away, and I caught a vision of Christ that set my soul on fire.

Then, what a difference! Knowing Him afresh and at firsthand, and with a sense of His love flowing through my whole being, my tongue became, as the Psalmist put it, 'the pen of a ready writer' (Psa. 45:1). I was the same person. I occupied the same pulpit. I said mostly the same things that I had said before, but the difference was this – before I had been merely saying something, now I had something to say.

Infected with secularism

A third reason why we are so lethargic and indifferent is this: *we have become infected with the secularism of the age*.

Some years ago, a speaker addressing a Christian conference challenged his hearers with this question: do we still believe that all men need to be saved or has the secularism of the world so seeped into our churches that it is tacitly accepted that to be decent is all we can reasonably ask of men?

These words, spoken over two decades ago, are equally applicable to our contemporary Christian society. Although there is a rising tide of evangelism in today's church, there are still large sections of the Christian community where it is believed that salvation comes through human effort. The truth is that man is utterly incapable of saving himself, now or at any time in the future.

I heard recently of three ministers in the north of England who resigned their pulpits on the grounds that they could no longer preach the Gospel as it was expected of them by their churches and by their denomination. These ministers, all of whom went through theological training together, said, when questioned by a newspaper reporter: 'We do not feel it right to ask people for a clear testimony to Christian conversion before they can be admitted to the fellowship of the Church. Men and women are dear to God by reason of His image which has been stamped into them. All He requires is but the faintest desire to be better, and on this basis men and women are welcomed into His fold.'

Now while I cannot agree with the conclusions of these men, I certainly admire their honesty and integrity in resigning their position as leaders of their congregations. What grieves me is the fact that there are literally hundreds of churches where, Sunday after Sunday, ministers continually contradict the Scripture by insisting that men and women are capable of saving themselves and providing their own redemption. Such men are not servants of Christ but agents of the devil!

This age has done much to make human existence more tolerable. Modern-day science has almost wiped out killer diseases like tuberculosis and smallpox. Slowly but surely a society steeped in secularism has come to deny the existence of God, and believe that man can save himself.

Our position as true Christians is the exact opposite of this. We affirm the existence of God and deny that unaided man can ever find peace in his soul. It is no part of my purpose to denigrate the secular society or to disparage the achievements of modern science and technology. I am thankful for all the advancements this age has brought, but there is one thing society cannot do and that is make a sinner into a saint.

We Christians must examine our hearts. Are we loyal to our central message? Do we apply it faithfully and fearlessly in today's secular society? Do we believe that *all* men need to be saved, and saved not from stupidity, but sin? God forgive us, if, failing to make that message clear, we have encouraged men and women to think that salvation is by human effort alone, and that there is no great loss to those who do not bow the knee to the Lord and Saviour Jesus Christ.

Personal problems

A further reason why Christians are reluctant to share their faith is *because of the pressure of their own personal problems*. 'I have so many problems of my own,' they say, 'I would feel like a hypocrite telling others that Christ can solve their problems.'

John White, a Christian psychiatrist, writing on this point, says:

'Has it never dawned upon you that the essence of witnessing is just plain honesty? You are salt – whether you feel like it or not. You are not told to act like salt but to be what you are. You are a light. God has done a work in your life. Don't try to shine. Let the light that God put there shine out. It demands no more than honesty. It demands honesty before unbelievers. In fact such honesty is ninety percent of witnessing. Witnessing is not putting on a Christian front so as to convince prospective customers. Witnessing is just being honest, that is, being true to what God has made you in your speech and everyday behaviour.'

Non-Christians know we are not perfect, and if we pretend to have no problems, when we do, then they will pick up and detect our dishonesty.

Recently, in a church where I had spoken about the need to be open and honest in our relationships with everyone, a young girl came up to me after the service and said, 'I would like to share with you something that happened to me a little while ago that will illustrate the importance of what you have been saying tonight.' Although I cannot quote her words verbatim, the following is very close to what she said:

'I am a college student – eighteen years of age. For a year I shared a room in college with another girl whom I constantly tried to win to Christ. One of my strategies in witnessing was to present the fact that once Christ comes into our lives then He solves all our problems, and we no longer have anything to worry us. I knew, however, that what I was saying was not entirely true because I was deeply disturbed about many things, and I was not actually experiencing the truth of what I was saying. My room mate obviously picked up the dishonesty of my approach, even though she couldn't put her finger on it, and one night she confronted me with the fact that there was something phony about my Christian witnessing.

'She said, "If Christ has solved all your problems then why do you walk around with your brow furrowed, looking like someone you loved just died?" This brought me up with a jolt. I realised that in my effort to present Christ as the solver of every problem, I was living under a great strain. He hadn't solved all of my problems – and it was showing.

'When my friend confronted me with the reality of my behaviour, I broke down and wept. I shared with her the reasons why I had presented things the way I had, and told her of the many problems I was grappling with which seemed to have no clear resolution. For a while, she said nothing, but then at last she turned to me and remarked, "For the first time in over a year I know you are a real person. Now I'm willing to listen to what you have to say about your faith." '

The young girl went on to say that this new openness and honesty brought about such a climate of change between herself and her room mate that a few months later she had the joy of leading her friend into a personal experience of Christ.

Fear of Rejection

Yet another reason why people are reluctant to share their faith is *fear of rejection*. A young nurse once wrote to me saying, 'I feel an urge to share my faith at appropriate times and in appropriate places, but whenever I try to tell others of Christ something rises within me to block my words and statements. Will you help me trace this problem to its roots?'

I set up a special appointment with the young woman, and after several hours of discussion, we came to see that her basic problem was a fear of rejection. This young woman, like so many others I have known, was unable to share her faith effectively because she wasn't able to cope with the feelings that stirred within her when confronted by indifference or downright hostility.

The fear of rejection has roots which go deep down into the personality. This is not the place to focus on the psychological reasons for such a fear but believe me, through the power of the Holy Spirit and by adopting the right attitude, this fear can be overcome.

I intend to focus a little later on upon the work and involvement of the Holy Spirit in Christian witness, so at this stage I want to draw your attention to the importance of what is sometimes called 'self-talk'. Dr Albert Ellis claims that one of the major reasons why we feel negative emotions is a direct result of our belief system – what we tell ourselves. He has put his views into a formulae known as the ABC theory of emotion.

A equals the activating event.

B equals the way we evaluate or perceive that event.

C equals the consequent emotion.

For example, I witness to someone about Christ and they react in hostility so I feel deeply rejected. But (according to Ellis) there is no way that a person's rejection of Christ can make me feel deeply rejected. I may feel hurt, or somewhat saddened, but if I feel personally rejected then it is because the B part of the formula is wrong: I am evaluating the situation from a wrong perspective.

The way to overcome the problem is to address the B in the formula (my evaluations and perceptions) with proper self-talk.

The apostle Paul, I believe, understood this subject very clearly. In several places he reminds us that the work of self-control begins in our minds. In 2 Corinthians 10:3–5, he shows us that the battle is not taking place so much in the external environment (the A's) as in our minds (the B's). We are to 'destroy arguments and every proud obstacle to the knowledge of God, and take every thought captive to obey Christ' (RSV). We are to capture these thoughts, change them and bring them into obedience to Christ.

How do we do that?

Paul answers that question for us in Philippians

4:8. Every thought that enters our mind is to be examined in the light of this verse. We are urged to think about whatever is true, honourable, just, pure, lovely or gracious, 'if there is any excellence, if there is anything worthy of praise, think about these things' (RSV). And the promise is that 'the God of peace will be with you'.

So if fear of rejection is your problem, then begin to talk to yourself – in Biblical terms. Focus on such Scriptures as these:

'Blessed are those who are persecuted – for theirs is the kingdom of heaven' (Matt. 5:10, RSV).

'Blessed are you when men revile you . . .' (Matt. 5:11, RSV).

On the basis of these texts (and there are many more), say to yourself something like this: 'I shall naturally feel disappointed when others reject me for my witness to Jesus Christ. But I need not let this devastate me. If my life is so inextricably bound up with Christ, then rejection of Christ will mean rejection of me. It cannot be otherwise. If I feel devastated by my experience, then this is because there are roots of insecurity in me which this is touching. I shall let Christ heal these roots and fears, and shall recognise that this problem needs to be brought out into the open and faced. The problem is not in Him or in the person, but in me. I will overcome it in His Name.'

When you change your thinking, as Paul says in Romans 12:1–2, you change your life. Try it and see!

3: The art of communication
or
What was that I never heard you say?

Eyes shut tight, a little boy was finishing his bedtime prayer. 'Bless Mummy and Daddy,' he said, 'and please, Harold . . . please make Grandma better.' His mother gasped, 'Why did you say "Harold" '? she asked. 'Who's that?'

Her son looked up surprised. 'Why, don't you know?' he said. 'That's God. We learned his name in Sunday School. 'Our Father who art in heaven . . . Harold be thy name . . .'

The little boy's mother had stumbled on an error of communication that was simple to correct. But some of our failures in this important field are not so simply remedied.

How tragic that in an age which is witnessing a 'communication explosion', we Christians, who are called by God to pass on the most important truths in history, fail to get our message home. Sometimes we are misunderstood or we say things we never meant to say. More often than not, we fail to pass on anything. And that's an even bigger problem.

When novelist Ann Rand was interviewed by a reporter from *Time* magazine some years ago, she was asked this pointed question: what's wrong with the modern world? Her reply was one of the most penetrating and incisive statements of modern times. She said, 'Never before has the world been so desperately asking for answers to crucial questions, and never before has the world been so frantically committed to the idea that no answers are possible.'

'To paraphrase the Bible,' she continued, 'the modern attitude is "Father, forgive us, for we know not what we are doing – *and please don't tell us.*" '

It is to such a generation that God has called us to relate – a generation searching for answers it doesn't really believe are there. Obviously, if we are going to get through, we have to construct clear lines of communication. We cannot, indeed we dare not, cloud or fog the message.

The components of communication

Nothing is more difficult than communicating. Talking is easy, but communicating is hard work. Howard Hendricks says, 'If you find yourself talking more and enjoying it less you may be on the verge of the greatest breakthrough in your life and ministry. Nothing is as easy as talking: nothing is as difficult as communicating.'

A man once told a Christian counsellor in a marriage guidance session that his wife talked too much. 'And what does she talk about?' asked the counsellor. 'That's the trouble,' replied the man, 'she doesn't say!' If we are to reach this generation for Jesus Christ then we must do more than just say something – we must make sure we get our message across.

In recent years a good deal of research has gone into the subject of communication. Experts claim that only seven percent of communication flows through our words. Thirty-eight per cent is communicated by our tone of voice. And fifty-five per cent is conveyed by the non-verbal signals we use, sometimes called 'body language'.

If we tell someone that God loves them, the words we use, though carefully chosen, comprise just seven per cent of the communication process. What gives the message meaning is the tone of voice we use. That complements the message (say the experts) by another thirty-eight percent. But there is something that complements the words in an even more powerful way – body language. By body language, I mean such things as facial

NON-VERBAL
55%

TONE OF VOICE
38%

ACTUAL
WORDS
7%

expression, posture, dress, gesticulation and so on.

When these three components of communication complement each other, then the message stands a greater chance of getting through. If, however, the words we speak are contradicted by our tone of voice and body language, then this is what is called a 'contradictory message'. And the words, however carefully constructed and however meaningful, will have far less impact.

A few days ago I stood at a check-out counter in the local supermarket with my wife. We had purchased several items one of which was not marked-up and the cashier was obliged to ring for a supervisor to check the price. At this point, a woman, standing in line behind us, seemed to be getting agitated, and the cashier, sensing this, said, 'I'm sorry to keep you waiting, Madam. I'm sure this won't take long.'

'Oh, that's all right,' replied the woman. 'I've plenty of time.'

Unfortunately, however, the woman's tone of voice and body language contradicted her statement, giving my wife and me the impression that all was not as well as it sounded. She spoke through clenched teeth, her eyes flashed in anger and she moved impatiently from one foot to the other. The luckless cashier picked this up too, and in an effort to speed up the process, he made several serious accounting mistakes which had to be corrected.

After a few minutes, the woman behind us threw down her few packages on the counter and stormed out of the store. 'What's wrong with her?'

said the cashier to my wife and me. 'I thought she said that she had plenty of time!'

I remarked to my wife when we were outside the store, 'It's sometimes better to listen to what people say by their body language than what they say by their words – you get a truer message.'

Let's examine the components of communication in greater detail, for I believe that when we understand these three simple principles underlying communication, and begin to put them into practice, we can, with the help of the Holy Spirit, greatly enhance our evangelistic endeavours.

1. Words comprise just seven percent of a message

Because words make up only seven percent of a message, we must not run away with the idea that the words we use are unimportant. The Bible has a good deal to say about the power of words. 'Death and life,' says the writer of Proverbs, 'are in the power of the tongue' (Prov. 18:21).

When God created the world He did it by words.

'In the beginning God created the heaven and the earth . . . And God *said*, 'Let there be light' and there was light' (Gen. 1:1,3).

God's words produced a world – a world of beauty and harmony. When we speak, we, too, create a world – a cosmos or a chaos. What kind of world are *we* creating by our words?

Speak in language that is clearly understood. The apostle Paul focuses on an interesting communication problem in 1 Corinthians 14:8 when he says: 'And if the army bugler doesn't play the right notes, how will the soldiers know that they are being called to battle?' (TLB). Similarly, if you talk to a person in words he doesn't understand, how will he know what you mean?

A minister, who was well-known for his work in the air raid shelters during the London Blitz in the Second World War, recalls overhearing a conversation between a Christian woman and a down and out.

'The conversation,' he said, 'had been going on for some time when it fell upon my startled ear that she was saying, "You know it must be yea and amen to all the promises of God . . . I suspect you are still living under the old dispensation . . . I am not sure you understand the difference between natural and effectual faith . . . I wish you could experience a mighty outpouring of the Holy Spirit . . . You do realise, don't you, that all your righteousness is as filthy rags?" '

'The down and out,' said the minister, 'took little part in the conversation. When the woman finally left him, murmuring something about making intercession for him at the throne of grace, the man's rather comical reply was: "Okey, dokey!" '

Two worlds converged in those two persons, but they did not meet. Her language had gone over his head.

If you have to use words like 'atonement' or 'redemption', then explain what they mean. Missionaries learn the language of the natives to whom they minister, and Christians who stay at home must learn to speak in everyday terms to people.

Speak more about Christ than you do about your-

self. Personal testimony is good, but many Christians would be startled if their evangelistic conversations were played back on a tape recorder, and they heard how much of their testimony focused on themselves rather than on Christ. '*I* was this . . . *I* did that . . . *I* am now like this.'

I am not saying one should refrain from giving a personal testimony. It is fine to illustrate the difference which Christ has made in your life, but talk of self should be the undertone, the stress should fall on the Master.

In Westminster Abbey there is a section known as Poet's Corner. Many visitors to that part of the Abbey take a particular dislike to the memorial to John Milton. It reads thus:

> *In the year of our Lord Christ*
> *One thousand seven hundred thirty and seven*
> *This Bust*
> *of the author of PARADISE LOST*
> *was placed here by William Benson Esquire*
> *One of the two Auditors of the Imprest*
> *to his Majesty King George the Second*
> *formerly*
> *Surveyor General of the Works*
> *to his majesty King George the First*
> *Rysbrack*
> *Who was the Statuary who cut it . . .*

One visitor to Poet's Corner says, 'When my eye first fell on that memorial, I read it twice. "Who is it all about?" I asked myself in bewilderment. Then I got it! It is all about William Benson! He put up the memorial as a device to get his own unimportant name noticed. Milton is merely the excuse!'

Sometimes when I have listened to some Christians sharing the Gospel with the unconverted, this device of William Benson, who used the name of a Puritan poet to bring himself into the public gaze, has come to mind. They seem to want to make more of themselves than they do of Christ.

The root of the problem is spiritual pride. One has wanted to remind them of the words of John the Baptist: 'He must increase, but I must decrease' (John 3:30). Make it a rule, when witnessing, to say seven words about Christ for every word you say about yourself.

Speak words that befit your status as an ambassador of Jesus Christ. Paul told the Colossian converts: 'Let your speech be always with grace' (Col. 4:6).

The word 'grace' is a theological word which describes God's kindness and favour which is freely bestowed upon us in Christ. When used of our speech, it simply means that we employ words that are kind and gracious. When we do this, our words will give grace to those who hear us (Eph. 4:29). Other terms are used in the New Testament to convey the need for gracious words.

'Let no foul or polluting language, nor evil
words, nor unwholesome or worthless talk
ever come out of your mouth, but only such
speech as is good and beneficial to the spiritual
progress of others, as is fitting to the need and
the occasion that it may be a blessing and give

grace (God's favour to those who hear it)' (Eph. 4:29, Amplified Bible).

'And let your instruction be sound and fit and wise and wholesome, vigorous and irrefutable and above censure so that the opponent may be put to shame finding nothing discrediting or evil to say about us' (Titus 2:8, Amplified Bible).

I was once asked by the elders of a church, which at that time was without a pastor, if I would talk to one of the members whose task it was to organise house to house visitation.

A problem had arisen because some of the church members who assisted him in house to house visitation felt that he was misrepresenting the cause of Christ through improper language.

The dear fellow, a retired miner, felt it would be useful in his evangelistic encounters to show people that he was just like everyone else, and so he used words that, to say the least, were somewhat vulgar and indecent. This, he thought, made him one of them, and gave him an immediate entrance into their hearts.

When I spoke to him about the issue of identifying with sinners yet being different from them, he saw the point and immediately took steps to prune and purify his vocabulary.

As Christ's ambassadors we have a responsibility to select our words carefully and use only those that befit our ambassadorial status.

2. *Tone of voice makes up thirty-eight percent of a message*

I am writing this chapter at the end of what we in Britain called 'The Falklands Crisis'. Almost daily during the crisis, we saw the face of Ian MacDonald, the Defence Ministry spokesman, on our television sets. His task was to give us the facts concerning the progress of the British Forces in the Falklands battle. He spoke deliberately, unemotionally and soberly. His tone of voice matched the messages he gave, and the British people gathered from his communications that the situation was, indeed, grave.

His tone of voice was, of course, quite appropriate for the messages he conveyed, but I could hardly imagine Ian MacDonald presenting the Gospel in the same way. The message of the Gospel is a message of Life – Life with a capital L! And when we share it, we must share it in a tone of voice that matches its content.

A minister I know, a lecturer in a theological college, tells his students: 'Whenever you share the Gospel with anyone *get excited for God's sake.*'

Go to Hyde Park on a Sunday afternoon and watch the rabble rousers! They share their message with unashamed enthusiasm. It's not what they say that arrests people's attention, but the way they say it. A right use of words is important in communicating, but it is not enough. The tone of voice we use has a marked effect upon the meaning of our words.

Many years ago, someone asked the great British preacher, C. H. Spurgeon: 'How can I communicate like you?'

'It's very simple,' he said, 'Get on fire for God and the people will come to see you burn!'

He meant, of course, that when a herald of Christ's message is *fired* from within by the meaning of the message, then it will not be long before he captures the attention and interest of others. And the more excited he becomes about the wonder of the Gospel, the more it will affect his tone of voice.

Try saying 'Jesus loves you' in a dull and indifferent tone of voice. Go ahead – say it aloud. Notice how your tone of voice detracted from the beauty of those three words? Now say it again, but this time in a tone that matches the words. Say it aloud, excitedly, 'Jesus loves you!' Can you see the point I am making?

This was vividly illustrated to me in my teenage years by a man in the village in South Wales where I was brought up whose name was Dewi Morgan. Dewi was my Sunday School teacher, and did as much as anyone to bring me to Christ. Unfortunately, he suffered from a slight speech impediment. Because he stumbled over his words, he had learned to cut his sentences short, sometimes to just three or four words.

I can remember his telling me on numerous occasions: 'God loves you . . . He wants you for Himself . . . He died for you . . . Give Him your life . . .' and so on.

The thing that remains in my memory to this day is the tone of voice Dewi used when he spoke to me concerning the state of my soul. It was tender, compassionate, loving, concerned, winsome and considerate. There were times when I brushed his arguments aside, but there was no way I could defend against his tone of voice. At times it haunted me. I would wake up in the middle of the night and hear the words, 'God loves you,' spoken in such tender tones.

And when finally I walked down the aisle of the church in the village of Fochriw, Glamorganshire, to receive Christ, my conversion was due in no small measure to the impact that Dewi's compassionate tone of voice had made upon my life.

Dewi has now gone to be with the Lord, and when I talked recently to a man who had come to know Christ through Dewi's life and witness, he told me, 'It wasn't what he said. It was the way he said it that got through.'

So when you next attempt to communicate the Gospel don't present your message as if you were reading the news. Meditate on the significance of the message until the wonder of it creeps into the tone of your voice. If it doesn't, believe me, the words you speak, however correct and true, will largely be lost. Communication means getting through to people. So clothe your words in the appropriate tone of voice.

3. Non-verbal language makes up fifty-five percent of the message.

Although our words and our tone of voice make up a large part of our message, it is greatly enhanced by the non-verbal signals we send out to people. Body language (according to the experts) is even more powerful than our words and our tone of voice.

But what exactly is non-verbal communication, or body language as it is sometimes called?

Non-verbal communication is the way we communicate apart from our words. It includes such things as the way we use our eyes, our hands, our feet and so on.

When I was a small boy with a strong propensity towards misbehaviour, I could sometimes read the message in my father's eyes from across the other side of a room. The message I often picked up was this: 'Behave yourself . . . or else . . .' My sister and I used to refer to my father's non-verbal messages as 'Dad's beady eye'. *Looks* can communicate.

A few months ago I had an opportunity to witness a situation in which a sincere and well-meaning Christian failed to communicate with an apparently earnest seeker of salvation. It happened during an evangelistic crusade I was conducting in one of Britain's sea-coast towns. I use this illustration, not to denigrate the person concerned, but to show how the wrong non-verbal signals can contradict and sabotage what is being conveyed in the other two areas of communication.

Following the presentation of the Gospel in an evangelistic meeting, it is my custom to invite those who would like to receive Christ to walk forward as an act of public commitment. Following this, they are then taken into a specially prepared counselling room where local Christians are on hand to pray with them and help clarify their spiritual commitment.

One night after the service, I walked into the counselling room and stood not far from a woman counsellor who was seated at a table, talking to a girl of about eighteen years of age.

I noticed that as the counsellor spoke to the girl, she leaned forward, looked interested and intent and spoke with great enthusiasm. I was impressed. However, when the girl responded by sharing some of her problems, the counsellor leaned back in her chair, allowed her gaze to wander round the room and looked uninterested. Then, when it was her turn to speak, she leaned forward again and spoke with apparent warmth and enthusiasm. This happened several times. When it was the counsellor's turn to speak, she would be the picture of warmth and enthusiasm, but when the young girl responded, the counsellor leaned back, looked around the room and tapped her foot impatiently.

This is what psychologists call devaluing a person. The counsellor was saying by her words and tone of voice, 'I am concerned about you and want to lead you to a saving knowledge of Jesus Christ.' However, by her non-verbal language, she was saying, 'Hurry up and make your spiritual commitment, then all your problems will come right.'

I was greatly relieved when the leader of the counselling team, recognising that the counsellor was in difficulty, tactfully intervened. Within minutes, he had the girl at her ease and communicated with her in a way that helped to affirm, not devalue her, as a person.

The counsellor, I know, acted out of ignorance, but I can't help wondering how many evangelistic encounters fail because the Christian witness doesn't know how to present a complemetary message.

A friend of mine who attended a School of

Evangelism in a European city, described to me one of the ways in which the students were taught the power of non-verbal communication. They were sent out to walk the streets of the city and told to spend fifteen minutes smiling at people and fifteen minutes scowling at people. They were then asked to return to the lecture room to share their experiences.

Those who took part in the experiment said that when they smiled at people, people mostly smiled back, some even responding with a word of greeting. When they scowled, however, the people mostly turned the other way, crossed to the other side of the street, or made a rude remark.

Jesus in the Sermon on the Mount said, 'Others will treat you as you treat them' (Matt. 7:2, TLB).

Psychologists are now calling this the *Law of Reciprocity*. Those who study the laws underlying human relationships are seeing that just as Jesus taught, each person takes his cue on how to behave from the people he meets.

So if you send out the message that you are interested in getting a person to make a decision for Christ, but your non-verbal language shows that you are not interested in him as a person, then he may not show all that much interest in your message.

Non-verbal communication is not a 20th century phenomenon. The Bible talks a good deal about it. Take, for example, 'the right hand of fellowship' given to Paul and Barnabas when they began their ministry to the Gentiles (Gal. 2:9). Or what about the exhortation to greet one another with 'a holy kiss' (1 Cor. 16:20). The look that Jesus gave Simon Peter spoke more powerfully than

48

any words (Luke 22:61), and the act of washing another's feet said something concrete and wonderful about servanthood (John 13:14).

So remember, in order to communicate you must make sure that your non-verbal language complements, not contradicts, what you are saying. Non-verbal communication, if expressed properly, can powerfully enhance your verbal sharing.

You can:

– lean forward in your seat
– nod sympathetically
– open your arms rather than keeping them folded
– keep your gaze fixed on the person
– look interested
– refrain from crossing and uncrossing your legs
– make sure your breath is not offensive

'The language of God's Good News must travel a straight course,' says one preacher, 'if spiritually dead lives are to be made alive in Christ.'

He added:

'Christian communication is like a blunderbuss,
We fire a monstrous charge of shot
And sometimes hit,
But mostly not.'

It's time to put away the blunderbuss and get on target!

4: Caring enough to listen

Even though it happened over thirty years ago, I can still remember the afternoon when a friend and I set out to do some evangelistic work on a housing estate in the city of Bristol. I was a student at a theological college there at the time, and after a morning lecture on the subject of evangelism, we were sent out in two's into the local area to meet people in their homes and witness to them about Jesus Christ.

My companion was a young Frenchman, Andre Lemarquand, a brilliant design artist once in a career with Walt Disney now training to become a full-time minister of Jesus Christ.

Our technique was to knock at a door, explain that we were theological students from a college in the area, and then take it in turns to give a simple evangelistic presentation.

At one house, a lady in her late thirties appeared at the door, and as it was my turn to speak, I at once launched into my spiel:

'Christ came two thousand years ago to this earth to die on a cross for you,' I said, 'and unless you repent and turn to Him you will be lost for all eternity.'

Hardly pausing for a breath, I rattled off a few more prepared statements, when suddenly my friend Andre interrupted my flow by saying to the woman: 'Excuse me, is there something bothering you? Can we do anything to help?'

I remember feeling a little irritated with Andre. Why should he interrupt my presentation in this way? What crass insensitivity, I thought to myself.

The woman looked hesitantly at Andre and me, but after a few moments, she invited us in. We were hardly seated before she began to pour out her troubles. Her teenage children were causing her great difficulty, her mother was desperately ill and dying, and she was finding it difficult to make ends meet financially. During the twenty minutes or so we simply sat and listened.

Taking my cue from Andre, I restrained myself from finishing my prepared evangelistic speech, and focused upon her, not as a potential 'fish' to be landed, but as a person with fears, apprehensions and problems.

After listening to her, we prayed together, and left her with an invitation to attend some evangelistic meetings being held at that time by Howell Harris, a Welsh evangelist.

Several nights later we had the joy of seeing her and one of her daughters walk forward at the end of an evangelistic service to receive Christ as their Lord and Saviour. As we counselled them both, the woman said, 'You will never know what you did for me that afternoon when you listened to my problems. No one had ever listened to me with such concern before. I don't think I would have been here tonight were it not for the love of Christ I saw in you that afternoon.'

Listening – an important aspect of evangelism

I owe it to my friend Andre for helping me to see the importance of sensitive listening. I took the position of salesman with a gift to offer – a product to sell – but I did not sense the silent plea of the customer. Andre, by showing he was interested in the woman as a person and was willing to listen to her problems, paved the way for a deep work of the Holy Spirit to take place. After we had listened to her, she was then more ready to listen to us.

In many of our evangelistic efforts, do people fail to listen to us because we have not first listened to them?

Have you ever been witnessing to a person and sensed that their thoughts are a million miles away? Well, this person may still be reeling from a row with his wife that morning, or perhaps a business deal has gone wrong.

Now when I encounter a person who I think is inwardly hurting, I encourage him to talk. This shows I am interested in him as a person, and I may get the chance to really help. This approach must not be used as a device. We must genuinely care for people and their problems, and see them not merely as potential converts, but as men and woman we can help.

One of the most important skills in modern-day evangelism is learning how to listen. Too often we try to 'sell' Christ to others. We streamline our verbal approach, learn how to handle difficult questions, work at overcoming resistance; we try to 'collect' decisions for Christ. When we use this salesmanship method of communicating the

Gospel, we forget that: (a) communication is two-way and (2) new ideas are best communicated on the level of mutual trust and understanding. To communicate we must not only talk – we must *listen*.

But listening is not easy. You must be able to cut off all else going on around you and concentrate totally on the person in front of you. Consider some of the mistakes Christians make when listening to others during a time of witnessing.

Mistakes often made

One mistake is thinking about what you are going to say while the other person is still talking! If you do this, then you will become more conscious of yourself than you are of the other person, and your preoccupation will block you from listening perceptively. Someone has said that if you fail to focus fully on what a person is saying when he is talking to you, then you are not listening but *pretending* to listen.

Becoming preoccupied with your own thoughts, and failing to concentrate fully on what the other person is saying, really devalues that person. And not only that – it means that you will be sending out conflicting messages. You are saying that you want the person to share his deepest needs with you, but your eyes, posture and facial expression will be saying something else. Your body language will be saying: 'Shut up, so that I can take charge and tell you what I want you to do.'

Another mistake people make when listening is to prejudge people by assuming they know what their answers mean. I once overheard a Christian witnessing to a non-Christian on a park bench in the town of Colchester in Essex.

The Christian said to the non-Christian: 'Have you considered the importance of being ready to meet your Creator and His Son, the Lord Jesus Christ?'

The non-Christian replied, 'I don't believe in Jesus Christ'.

Instantly, the well-meaning but greatly misguided Christian said, 'Then I am afraid, my friend, you are bound for a never-ending hell and a lost eternity.'

I hope you will never witness like that!

What was his mistake?

This.

He assumed that he knew what the other person meant when he said, 'I don't believe in Christ.'

Now ask yourself: what *could* that man have meant by such a statement? He could have meant: 'I don't believe that Christ ever lived.' Or: 'I believe Christ lived, but I don't place any great credibility in his words.' He could also have meant: 'I don't believe it is necessary to come to God through Christ.'

All kinds of possible answers lie buried in that man's statements, but the Christian failed to check out the true meaning. What he should have said is: 'Can you clarify for me what you mean by that statement, "I don't believe in Christ?" ' This would have given him the full information he needed to continue the conversation.

When witnessing, never assume what a person means by a statement. Check it out. If a statement is not absolutely clear, ask them to clarify it.

When you jump to conclusions, and prejudge issues, then you are proving you are not a good listener.

Yet another mistake people make when listening is letting their own ego needs intrude into the situation. In anything as personal as witnessing, it is very easy to let your own ego get in the way.

In a seminar on Evangelism I once conducted, a young man said, 'I'm a talker. I can't sit too long without saying something, and the more I think about it, the more I realise I get far more satisfaction from talking than I do from listening. Why should this be?'

I encouraged the young man to begin to look at his own ego needs. After thinking about this for a while, he came up with the interesting insight: 'Perhaps the way I get my feelings of significance is by being in control of a conversation.'

I encouraged him to explore it still further, and eventually he came to realise that the urge he felt deep within continually to express himself was a psychological one that needed to be resolved by Christ. When he surrendered this to the Lord, he was released from the inward pressure to perform, and after working on the principles of listening for a few weeks, he became an expert listener and effective at witnessing.

If you sense that your own ego needs are getting in the way of listening, then you need to sit down and examine your motives. Ask yourself: am I doing this to meet my own needs, or am I concerned about helping the other person meet his? If you find your ego intruding, then learn to put it on the shelf, so to speak, and be as humble as Jesus was when He washed the disciples' feet.

Listening, then, is:

* not thinking about what you are going to say when the other person has finished talking.
* not prejudging issues by assuming you know what a person's answer means.
* not letting your ego needs intrude into the witnessing process.

'Listening,' says Norman Wakefield, 'is a *ministry*.'

Remember when God approached King Solomon and invited him to ask for whatever he wanted? This was his response: 'Give thy servant an understanding heart' (1 Kings 3:9). Most translations use the words *understand* or *discerning*, but the Hebrew word literally means *hearing*. Solomon perceived that in order to be an effective servant of the Lord, he needed to be an effective listener. Why is listening so crucial?

Listening helps people feel understood

First, *listening to a person helps them feel understood*. And I don't just mean listening to a person's words, but listening to the *feelings* that lie beneath those words.

Jesse Nirenberg in his book *Getting Through to People* says: 'Conversation is the main vehicle for expressing feelings as well as ideas. And since feelings are continually looking for outlets, we can see that conversations are bound to be filled with feelings, some erupting and others edging their way out.'

When one learns how to listen, not only to words and ideas, but to the feelings that lie beneath those words and ideas, and reflects these feelings back to the person, then one has discovered the most effective route to their heart.

Several years ago I was on a flight from London to New York, during which I entered into conversation with a fellow passenger. He asked what I did, and when I told him I was a minister of the Gospel, I saw him wince. As we talked it became obvious to me that he was extremely hostile towards Christianity, and I wondered whether I could possibly enter his world in the few hours that we were together.

I made no effort to initiate conversation, but simply responded to what he was saying about his work and family with an occasional nod or a quiet, 'I see'. In my heart I prayed a prayer that went something like this: 'Help me, Lord, to see this man not merely as someone to be won to You, but as someone to be loved.'

My concern and interest in him as a person began, I believe, to have an effect upon him, for he began to share things with me which originally he had not intended. He told me that he had been brought up in a religious sect well-known for their legalistic approach to Christian doctrine, and that he had been forced by his parents to avoid such things as competitive games and going to the cinema.

'Sounds like you had a pretty frustrating childhood,' I said. He looked at me strangely, and after a few minutes pause, said, 'Yes, that describes it exactly — it *was* frustrating.'

Soon he began to share some deep personal problems which he was struggling with, and as he did, I sought to identify the feelings beneath his words, and reflect to him what I felt he was saying. I said such things as: 'That must have really hurt,' or 'You were pretty disappointed when that happened, I imagine.'

When he finished telling me his personal problems, he fell silent for a few minutes, then turning to me, he said, 'You really understand me, don't you?'

What caused him to make such a remark? I had not given him any advice. I had not attempted to resolve his problems. I had simply listened, sought to pinpoint the feelings beneath his words, and reflected them to him. And when that is done, carefully and sincerely, it never fails to assure a person that you really understand him.

Later, I had an opportunity to share with him the truths of the Gospel, which he received most openly. Having talked to me, he was now ready to listen to me.

When we parted company at the customs desk in J. F. Kennedy airport, New York, he said to me, 'When you said you were a minister, I seriously considered changing my seat. But I'm glad I didn't. I don't think I have ever enjoyed a flight so much. Thank you for being so caring.'

The point of this illustration is not to impress you with my sensitivity to people's needs (believe me, I'm not always as good at it as I would like to be!) but to show you that I could never have reached this man's heart had I not first tuned in to the feelings that lay beneath his words and reflected them to him.

Someone put it like this: 'When you really listen to a person's words, this brings you right up to the front door of their life. When, however, you listen to the feelings that lie beneath those words, and show the person that you have heard a deeper message than that which he is conveying through his words, then this brings you right past the front door and gives you a seat in his living room!'

Listening helps others understand themselves

Secondly *listening helps others to understand themselves*. All of us have a deep-felt need to communicate, and the interesting thing is that the more we communicate the deeper the level of self-understanding.

Sydney Jourard, a counsellor and a psychologist, says, 'No man can come to know himself except at the expense of sharing himself with another person.' The Christian who knows how to listen makes it possible for the other person to come to know himself better.

Dennis Borg puts this point most effectively in an article written in *Christianity Today* (March 1981), He said:

'The importance of listening cannot be over-emphasised with regard to evangelism. Many people reject the Gospel because it seems to run contrary to their convictions, or because they have an 'uneasy feeling' about it. When a person is allowed to get his feelings and objections out into the open two things happen.

First, the Christian has an opportunity to answer the arguments and objections he raises, and second, more important, the non-Christian is helped to see the strengths and weaknesses of his own position, which he may be putting into words for the first time. As he understands his own ideas better, he is then able to examine the claims of the Gospel and, under the Spirit's direction, to change his mind. This often occurs after many hours of attentive listening.'

This aspect of listening involves us in listening for a person's ideas and reflecting them back to him in a summarised form.

One time, when I was a minister of a church in the North of England, a university student came to see me to discuss some doubts he had about the Christian faith. One of his doubts concerned the resurrection of Christ, and as I listened intently, I tried to enter into his problem with him. I said, 'Let me see if I understand you correctly. You are saying that while you find it easy to accept the fact that Christ died as a substitute for the whole of mankind, you cannot conceive how a man who was dead for three days could return from the dead and walk about the streets of Jerusalem as if nothing had happened?'

He nodded agreement so I went on: 'And in addition to that, I hear you say the doctrine of the resurrection is a stumbling block to you because it stretches credulity to the point where you have to believe in a miracle.' When I uttered those last few words – 'where you have to believe in a miracle' – he gasped and said, 'I see it so clearly now. That's exactly what it demands of me – a faith that believes in miracles.'

A few minutes later, he knelt beside the desk in my study and accepted Jesus Christ as his Lord and Saviour.

What brought about his young man's readiness to commit himself to the Christian faith? I simply reflected to him the ideas which were in his mind in such a way that it helped to clarify his own thinking. I really added very little to what he had been thinking, except that, as I reflected his thoughts to him in this way, he came to understand his own ideas better, and saw right to the heart of his problem.

One reason why I'm convinced that listening is an important ministry is because I've discovered so often that careful listening and reflecting back is essential in helping a person see right to the heart of his difficulty.

Frequently what a person *thinks* is his problem is not the real one, but only a felt or perceived one. As he airs it with a perceptive listener, he begins to see other dimensions of which he was not aware, and which greatly influence him in coming to a decision or finding a solution.

Listening lets others know we care

Thirdly, *listening is essential in personal evangelism because when we listen to people, really listen, this lets others know that we care.* We Christians talk a lot about love, but we often fail to show it. And there is no better way of showing love for a person than by listening to him.

Have you ever considered the fact that one of

the greatest evidences of God's love for you is that He *listens* to you? Ponder that a moment. Isn't it incredible! The sovereign Lord of the universe listens to you and me when we talk to Him. The Psalms are full of statements which identify God's listening love and care.

Take Psalm 6. David's distress is evident as he pours out his heart to God: 'My bones are in agony. My soul is in anguish' (vv. 2–3: NIV). 'I am worn out with groaning; all night long I flood my bed with weeping and drench my couch with tears' (v. 6: NIV). God listens.

Every one of us cries out to be heard. God knew that we would have that need, and that is why He made us to live together with others. He designed us like Himself 'in His own image', and every time we listen, we reflect the likeness of the listening Father.

When you really listen to a person, you are saying in essence: 'I care about you. You are important to me . . . important enough to have my undivided attention. I want to share your hurts and problems, your strengths and weaknesses, your joys and sorrows, your doubts and fears.'

This kind of listening requires many things of us but, above all, it requires *acceptance*. Acceptance says to a person, 'I accept you as you are. You can be yourself with me and I will not reject you for it.'

This does not mean that you will agree with everything a person says to you, but any disagreement you may have in relation to that person's lifestyle or opinions must not interfere with your acceptance of him as a person.

Too often as Christian witnesses we give people

the impression we are out to change them. They pick up this attitude in us and rightly resent it. Our job is not to convert people, but to introduce them to Jesus Christ. He is the one who converts them.

One writer put it this way: 'Jesus Christ always accepts people as they are. He changes people *after* they come to know Him.'

This issue of accepting people as they are is one that many Christians stumble over. We approach people with the attitude: 'I want to change you,' rather than: 'I want to introduce you to someone who can meet your every need.'

Once when talking to a group of a hundred people about the principles of acceptance, I wrote on a blackboard the following statement:

'I am thinking of walking out on my wife. She seems to have lost all interest in me, and I am convinced there is no way our love can be restored.'

I then asked the group to write down what their response would be to someone who made that statement to them during the course of a conversation. Only five out of the hundred gave the right answer. The rest said things like: 'You must give it another try.' 'Have you prayed enough about the matter?' 'Don't you know what the Bible says about the subject of separation and divorce?' 'I believe you ought to see a Christian counsellor.'

If I had some deep personal problems, I would hate to be counselled by people who responded to me in that way.

Don't misunderstand me. I am not saying that

there are never times when one has to lay down moral principles, or command a person to follow Biblically-based behaviour, or confront them with the reality of their lifestyle, but such judgments must never be the *initial* response to such a statement.

The five people who gave the right answer said something like this: 'Sounds like you feel pretty hurt and rejected at the moment.' 'I would imagine you must be feeling pretty desperate.' 'I think if I was in your position I would be feeling very frustrated.'

Just think of it! Only five people out of a hundred had the sensitivity to accept the man as he was. The others wanted to change him *before* they accepted him. Responses such as the other ninety-five gave are quite valid at a later stage of the conversation, but they are detrimental rather than helpful in the listening process.

Listening does not mean that a Christian witness is not to say anything. The Gospel, as we know, is Good News and has to be told. But as we have seen from the previous chapter, if the attitude of the messenger does not measure up to the quality of the message, then the message itself can be misunderstood and rejected.

Once you have listened intently to another person's point of view, and have shown that you understand them by reflecting their ideas and feelings back to them, then and only then have you earned the right to become an advocate for Christ.

Because you have listened in a way that regrettably few Christians do, your non-Christian friend will most likely follow the *Law of Reciprocity*, and listen to you. *This* is when you recommend Christ as the answer to their problems. They now see you as a loving, supportive friend, who is deeply concerned about their well-being, and that can mean far more than words in reaching a positive decision for Jesus Christ.

Witnessing is sharing the truths of the Gospel. Listening is the sharing of ourselves. And when it comes to making effective 'introductions' to Jesus Christ, there is no separation of the two.

5: Five keys to building relationships

Ever wondered why it is that certain people seem to relate to others without any difficulty? They are easy to talk to, skilful at developing conversation and appear to have a built-in capacity for good inter-personal relationships.

And such people are not always the good-looking types, the highly intelligent or outgoing. I have met many shy and ordinary people who despite their introverted temperament draw others to them like iron filings to a magnet.

What is it that makes people effective in the area of inter-personal relationships? Is it a special ingredient which is in their personalities from birth? With some it would seem so, but most people develop it by paying attention to the laws of relationships.

Yes, there are laws of relationships just as there are laws of physics. And, generally speaking, those who relate well to others do so because they work with the relationship laws. They have mastered what in this chapter we are going to call the 'R Factor' – the principles of good relationships.

My work as a Christian counsellor has furnished

me with a window on the way human beings relate to each other. I have talked to, and watched, thousands of people at different levels of their relationships, and over the years I have been able to observe what works and what does not work. And what I have discovered I want to share with you in this chapter.

Contact: the first four minutes

According to Leonard and Natalie Zunin, co-authors of the book *Contact: the first four minutes*, the way two people communicate during the first four minutes of contact is so crucial that it will determine the way the relationship will continue. They refer to it as breaking the four-minute barrier.

After careful study and research, they claim that when two people meet, there is a short segment of time – four minutes – during which initial contact is established or reaffirmed. Why *four* minutes? It is not an arbitrary interval. Rather, it is the average time that it takes to decide to part or continue their encounter.

By watching hundreds of people at parties, in schools and in churches, they discovered that four minutes is approximately the minimum breakaway point – the socially acceptable period that precedes a potential shift of conversational partners. They stress, of course, that because people are human beings and not machines, the four minutes is an average segment of time, both real and symbolic.

For some people getting through that four-minute barrier might sound as complicated as a supersonic aircraft breaking the sound barrier. But learning and practising a few simple relational skills can enable you to not only make contact with people, but stay in contact with them during the whole of your conversation.

What are some of the more important relational skills that we must learn if we are to relate effectively to those with whom we long to share our faith? Let me identify them.

1. Be yourself

When I urge you to improve your relationship skills, I am not suggesting that you change your personality.

A year or so ago a woman said to me: 'I am an introvert. Can you help me become an extrovert?'

Had she come to me with that question thirty years ago, when I first came into the Christian ministry, I probably would have attempted to do what she asked. But the longer I work with people, the more respect I have gained for the infinite complexity of the human personality. And the longer I live the more I realise that God has made each one of us special people. Our personalities, temperaments and backgrounds have equipped us to touch people in a way no one else could do. God wants us to use that specialness, and will work in us to produce the fruit and gifts of the Holy Spirit. The divine and human converge in our lives to produce a completely unique individual.

There is no one else in the world who can present the Gospel to others in exactly the same way that you can.

So I told the woman I had no desire or intention

68

of changing her into a garrulous and gregarious person. I explained it was not her introverted temperament that was causing her problems, but the lack of relationship skills. When she took the time and trouble to learn these skills, it didn't make her the life and soul of the party, but it did enable her to relate to people in a meaningful and effective way.

When I say 'be yourself', I am not saying that you take no steps to improve your personality. That, in a book of this nature, ought to go without saying. We owe it to God to change our bad habits for good ones, and to allow the fruit of the Spirit to reveal itself in our lives and characters.

Do you have the personality of an extrovert? Fine. Use it for God, but watch that you don't become overbearing and manipulative.

Do you have the personality of an introvert? That's fine too. But work on improving your conversational and relationship skills.

Your personality plays an important part in the communication process, because, as we saw, we communicate by what we are. Your personality becomes the lens through which the Holy Spirit focuses His truth, or, as one preacher puts it: 'No matter how clear or obscure your message, your personality shines through.'

God doesn't want you to be another Billy Graham or a Luis Palau. He wants you to be yourself. You are as different from anyone else as one blade of grass from another, and, for that reason, you are most attractive and effective when you are yourself. To be real is to be attractive, and you are least attractive when you try to be somebody else.

Remember Brother Lawrence? In his book *Practising the Presence of God*, he tells how one day, while working as a cook in a monastery, he discovered a thrilling spiritual secret. Day after day, through his kitchen window, he looked out on a beautiful tree. He thought to himself, 'In the cold of winter, the tree is dry and barren and unfruitful. As Spring comes, new life begins to come and buds appear. Then in summer the blossoms and the fruit comes. That tree is like my life.' He realised he could not build himself up into some kind of super personality for God to use. He could only trust God to work through him as he was. From that moment, Brother Lawrence rested in what he called 'practising the presence of God'.

So learn to rest in God, and recognise that as His life flows through the particular temperament and individuality which He has given you, you can share the faith with others in a unique and wonderful way.

Don't forget, God used some forty different authors to bring His complete revelation to mankind through the pages of the Bible. He poured His truth into them as they were, and as each contributed his own uniqueness, anointed by the Holy Spirit, God produced a composite picture of His love and purpose for the world. He will do the same things through your life and mine.

2. Accept people as they are

'One of the most effective ways of relating to people,' said Dr E. Stanley Jones, the famous missionary to India, 'is to accept people as they are, not as you would like them to be.'

In a study that was conducted some years ago in the United States, a number of psychiatrists, regarded by their peers and their patients as being particularly effective in their profession, were surveyed with the intention of finding out some of the ingredients of their success. In the list of qualities, one kept coming up time and time again. The men who were most successful had an ability to accept people as they were, and not as they would like them to be. In other words, they didn't pass judgment on people, but related to them just where they were.

Dr Paul Tournier, the Swiss medical doctor and counsellor has become so famous that many young doctors travel to Switzerland to learn his techniques. He said in one article: 'It is a little embarrassing for students to come over to study my techniques, for they always go away disappointed. *All I do is accept people.*' (Italics mine.)

Accepting people as they are and not as we would like them to be doesn't mean that we have to *approve* of everything they say or do. Acceptance is entirely a different matter. Some of the things I hear people say when I am involved in counselling are diametrically opposite to my own view of life and my understanding of Scripture. If I responded every time someone said something that ran counter to my views with such statements as: 'I don't believe that' . . . 'I don't agree with what you just said' . . . 'How could you do such a thing?' then the person would simply clam up, and whatever help I might try to give would not be easily received. Apart from that, I would be preparing myself for a nervous breakdown.

It is important that we learn to accept people as they are, and then attempt to lead them into what we consider God wants them to be – saved, sanctified and radiant Christian witnesses. If you feel compelled to render an immediate opinion about the things a person tells you, without first accepting the person as he is, then any attempt to share your faith will be blocked right from the start.

I've learned to listen to what people tell me without necessarily approving or disapproving. The best way to do that, of course, is by listening to a person's feelings. I help the person to understand that I accept his right to his views and his feelings. I make no mental judgment, for we are told in Scripture: 'Do not judge, or you too will be judged' (Matt. 7:1, NIV).

The more we learn to accept people as they are, and to listen to them without judging them, the more effective will be our ministry when it comes to the moment to point out the difference that being a Christian makes to life.

When you accept a person regardless of his lifestyle or even his sins, you are following in the footsteps of Jesus. I do not believe Christ approved of the prostitute's sin, the tax collector's greed or the other deficiencies He saw in people's characters. But He was able to differentiate between the sin and the sinner. And when we learn that secret, we have discovered one of the greatest keys to building relationships.

3. Don't try to do people good – love them

The great Indian poet and philosopher Tagore once said: 'He who tries to do people good stands knocking at the door, but he who loves finds the door wide open.'

I can remember in my pre-conversion days being stalked by a person intent on doing me 'good'. I avoided that person like the plague. But there were others who loved me for my own sake, and though I found their words challenging and confronting, I listened carefully to what they had to say. Few people can resist genuine love.

Howard Hughes (no relation of mine!) was one of the richest men in the world, yet he died of malnutrition. Hughes was married for thirteen years to Jean Peters, one of the most beautiful women in the world, but never in the whole of their married life were they ever seen together. They were divorced in 1970. 'As far as I know,' said a confidant of Hughes, 'he's never loved anyone. He has tried to do a lot of people 'good' but he knows nothing of love.'

Why was Hughes so isolated and bereft of friends? Why, with such unlimited wealth and hundreds of aides, was he so lonely? Simply because he chose to be. You will no doubt have heard the axiom: 'We use things and enjoy people.' However, it would appear that Hughes turned this around the other way – he enjoyed things and used people. Since his death many of his employees have talked of their contempt for him. They felt manipulated rather than appreciated.

In 1925 a hospital for mental patients opened in a place called Topeka, Kansas, USA. A team of physicians – a father and his two sons recently out of medical schools – determined to create a family atmosphere among their patients. The nurses were given specific instructions on how they were to behave towards their patients. 'Don't try to do them good – love them.' The young doctors concerned were Karl and Will Menninger, and today the Menninger Clinic has become world famous.

Karl Menninger said, 'Love is the medicine for the sickness of mankind. We can live if we have love.' So learn to love people – with supernatural love. It is a gift, of course, a gift from God. But it is freely given in response to importunate prayer.

4. Ask the right questions

Someone has said that 'questions are to a relationship what food is to living'. The way we ask questions of our acquaintances or friends determines to a great extent how effectively a relationship is built. Earlier I referred to Leonard and Natalie Zulin. In a section of their book *Contact: the first four minutes* they claim that one of the most effective ways of breaking the four-minute barrier is by a creative use of questions.

There are two different kinds of questions to be used: *fact* oriented questions and *feeling* oriented questions. Fact oriented questions relate to a person's family background, kind of work, areas of interest and so on. Such questions enable a person to relax as they do not demand too much thought or concentration to answer. Whenever I meet a person with whom I believe God wants me to share my faith, I begin by asking them a number of questions about themselves – their family, likes and dislikes, sport, etc. I try to demonstrate a genuine concern about the whole of their life, not just the salvation of their soul.

Examples of fact oriented questions are:

'What is your work?'
'Are you married or single?'
'Where do you live?'
'How long have you lived there?'
'What are your hobbies?'

These fact oriented questions supply you with information that you can use later in the conversation, and the answers you get will be a guide to what areas to explore as the conversation develops.

Feeling oriented questions are more personal and often more difficult to answer. They relate to a person's beliefs, value system, childhood experiences, view of life, and so on.

Examples of feeling oriented questions are:

'How do you feel about the teaching of the Bible?'
'Have you ever had a religious experience?'
'How do you feel about God?'
'Do you have any views on the subject of life after death?'

Remember, of course, to keep your feeling oriented questions open-ended. If you ask: 'Do you believe in God?' the person can answer with a simple yes or no. That might effectively end the conversation. You can stimulate the person's thinking much better by putting it in an open-ended form: 'How do you feel about God?'

Asking questions is not to be viewed as a device to get someone to open up to you spiritually. If you use them in that way then the person will soon catch on to what you are doing. Develop a genuine desire to know the person. It is far more important to demonstrate your understanding and desire to get to know the person than to impress him with your conversational brilliance or to overwhelm him with your knowledge of Scripture. Questions are to be used in learning to *understand* the person, and are the measure of your interest and concern.

But whatever you do, don't come across like a public opinion poll interviewer or a market research interviewer, firing questions and leaving hardly enough time for an answer! Questions must be asked gently, sincerely, and not in the style of a professional interrogator.

5. *Learn and remember a person's name*

You are most likely to hear a person's name within the first few minutes of meeting him or her. Remember it; use it several times in conversation. Most people will be flattered and impressed that you picked it up quickly, and according to a number of studies made on this subject, most people like to hear their names mentioned in a conversation. It makes them feel comfortable.

Calling someone by name indicates that you are interested in them, that you respect them and that you are aware of them as an individual.

When a person gives you their name, make sure you hear it clearly. If there is any doubt ask them to repeat it. If it is an unusual name, ask them to spell it for you. This will assist you in remembering it.

Some people find it difficult to remember names. This is usually due to lack of practice. So start right away to focus on people's names whenever you meet them. Emerson said that procrastination is the blight of the whole human species. 'I'll start tomorrow,' is the stock answer of the person who plans to go on a diet. Believe me, the more attention you pay to remembering and using someone's name, the more effectively you will be able to relate to that person.

Look at the way Jesus focuses on calling people by name.

'Simon son of John, do you truly love me more than these?' (John 21:15, NIV).

'Zacchaeus, come down immediately. I must stay at your house today' (Luke 19:5, NIV).

'Jesus said to her, "Mary" ' (John 20:16, NIV).

6. *Cultivate openness and transparency*

A famous psychiatrist was leading a seminar on the subject of getting patients to open themselves up. The psychiatrist challenged his colleagues with the statement: 'I can guarantee if you follow my technique that you can get a new patient to talk about the most private things during the first session without having to ask a question.'

What was his magic formula?

Simply this: he said that when a doctor began a session by revealing something personal about himself – his own fears, dislikes, antipathies, or something that was not common knowledge, this resulted in the patient being released to talk.

However questionable we may regard the doctor's technique, there can be no doubt about it that when a person takes the initiative in sharing themselves openly and honestly, the other person is more likely to respond in the same way. Obviously one would not want to take this principle as far as the psychiatrist suggested, but there is great value in adopting an open and transparent attitude when relating to others – it encourages them to open up in the same way to you.

Earlier I referred to Dr Paul Tournier. In one of his books he talks about a significant turning point in his career. It happened while he was practising as an intern in Geneva. He made contact with a small group of Christians who met together in a home for the purpose of sharing themselves openly and honestly. Although Tournier was a religious man at that time, he claims that his spiritual transformation took place in that group. People just shared themselves as they were, and spoke of their fears, joys, failures, disappointments and sometimes their sins.

He says that he developed such an attitude of transparency and openness in that climate, that when he returned to his medical practice he found people opening up to him in a way that he had not known before.

Why were they able to open up to him? Because he had cultivated such an air of openness that it came across to people non-verbally. They *sensed* when they talked to him that they were in the presence of someone who was undefensive, who had nothing to hide. And he found, as will you, that openness elicits openness.

Jesus, I believe, had this characteristic. He lived

out His life among His disciples, and shared Himself openly with them day by day. He broke bread with them, wept with them, prayed with them, helped them solve their arguments. He said on one occasion: 'I no longer call you servants, because a servant does not know his master's business. Instead, I have called you friends, for everything that I learned from my Father I have made known to you' (John 15:15, NIV).

When we encounter people who are transparent, we find it easy to dismantle our own defences. We can best learn to be transparent by sharing ourselves openly with each other in the Body of Christ, and the more we do that, the more open we become.

Openness and transparency does not mean, of course, that we have to 'let everything hang out', or that we reveal all that is on our minds. That would be foolhardy. Most people would fly from someone who wants to tell them their entire life story, with all its intimate details, in the first few minutes of becoming acquainted.

It simply means that when we learn to share ourselves openly and honestly, and cultivate an attitude of transparency, others will find it easier to relate to us.

7. Pay people compliments

In 1936 a book was published in in the USA that rocked the world. The author was an unknown YMCA instructor by the name of Dale Carnegie, who had left his job as a salesman to teach young people the principles of public speaking. Someone who listened to him suggested that he put the principles he was teaching into a book. He did and when *How to Win Friends and Influence People* hit the bookshops it was an immediate success. It stayed on the New York Times best-seller list for ten years, a record never since matched. The book has now sold over ten million copies, and continues to sell at about a quarter of a million copies a year.

One chapter of the book is entitled 'The Big Secret of Dealing with People', and this, said Dale Carnegie, is the pivotal point of his work. The big secret is simply this: 'Be hearty in your approbation and lavish in your praise.' Some, of course, have accused Dale Carnegie's techniques of being simplistic or downright manipulative, and there is no doubt that they have been used to manipulate people.

Once when he was speaking of passing on a compliment to someone, he was asked, 'What were you trying to get out of him?' This was his reply:

> 'What was I trying to get out of him? If we are so contemptibly selfish that we can't radiate a little happiness and pass on a bit of honest appreciation without trying to get something out of the other person in return . . . we shall meet with the failure we so richly deserve.'

So develop the habit of looking for something you can compliment a person upon soon after you have met them, or say something that affirms that person. It has a tremendously positive effect upon them.

I read recently of a minister, who was on a plane on his way to address a meeting in a certain city. He had been unable to get the Lord's mind on the message he was to give, and he hoped that the few hours of meditation on the plane would help clarify the issue: 'Oh God,' he prayed, 'help me. Give me something that will be useful to your people.'

But nothing came. He jotted down verses at random, feeling worse by the moment, and more and more guilty. During the course of the flight, a stewardess got into conversation with him, and happened to pay him a sincere and warm compliment. A few minutes later he realised that his whole attitude had changed. He felt uplifted and optimistic. Suddenly ideas flooded into his mind, and soon he had constructed a message that he knew instinctively was the right one for the people he was to address. He describes his change of attitude in these words:

' "God," I mused, 'how did this happen?' It was then that I realised someone had entered my life and turned a key. It was just a small key, turned by a very unlikely person. But that simple act of affirmation, that undeserved and unexpected attention, had got me back into the stream.'

The art of affirmation, of paying a person a sincere compliment, may sound to some more like a psychological device than a spiritual ministry.

Don't believe it! Jesus affirmed people. To Peter, the vacillating disciple, who seemed to go in the direction of any wind that blew, He said, 'You shall be a rock.' What a compliment! But then Jesus looked not only at the bad things about

81

people but the good things also. And He was not afraid to comment upon them.

God has put a key in your hands with which you can open the doors of a person's heart. Use it wisely. But *use* it. A simple act of affirmation may be the means, in God's hands, of opening up a person's heart to the truth of knowing God through His Son the Lord Jesus Christ.

6: Neglect this and watch your life wither

Just as there are certain principles which help us build relationships with people, so there are certain things we must do in order to build a relationship with God. In this chapter, I propose to look with you at some of the principles which, when practised, enable us to build a deeper and more meaningful relationship with our heavenly Father.

To me personally, one of the most challenging passages in the New Testament is found in the book of Jude, verses 20–23. I first discovered these verses a few weeks after I became a Christian, when God used them to motivate me to a deeper study of the Scriptures and a more intensive life of prayer.

The Holy Spirit has continued to bring these verses to my attention on scores of different occasions and I have come to regard them as one of the choicest and most challenging Scriptures in the whole of the Word of God.

Verse 20 in *The Living Bible* says: 'But you, dear friends, must build up your life ever more strongly upon the foundation of our holy faith, learning to pray in the power and strength of the Holy Spirit.'

The passage continues: 'Stay always within the boundaries where God's love can reach and bless you. . . . Try to help those who argue against you. Be merciful to those who doubt. Save some by snatching them as from the very flames of hell itself. And as for others, help them to find the Lord by being kind to them, but be careful that you yourselves aren't pulled along into their sins.'

That last clause – 'be careful that you yourselves aren't pulled along into their sins' – deserves close attention. You see, it is easy to so identify with sinners that you become identified with their sin. In other words, you can, unless you are extremely careful, be so concerned about winning people to Christ that you unwittingly cross the boundary line between righteousness and unrighteousness.

How can we protect ourselves from such a peril?

Spend time with God in the Bible

We can do it only by maintaining a close relationship with God, and one of the ways we can do that is by spending time with Him in the Bible – daily, if possible. I know some Christians claim that attempting to establish a system of daily Bible study is legalistic and brings one into spiritual bondage. I have not found it so myself.

I think a lot depends on the way one evaluates the Scriptures, and on one's convictions concerning the place and purpose of the Bible in a Christian's life. If a man or woman believes that the Bible is simply a book through which God spoke to His people in times past . . . well, the book will have little relevance to life now in the twentieth century. But if one believes, on the other hand, that God *speaks through the Bible to His people today*, then one will count any day incomplete which does not include some time given to its study and perusal.

The Bible after all is a unique volume. Whatever degree of divine inspiration may have gone into other Christian books such as *The Pilgrim's Progress* or *The Imitation of Christ*, no other book bears the imprint of God in the way the Bible does. And a book so divinely inspired needs divine help in order to be understood. That is why we must come to it with a prayer on our lips, that we might not only understand it, but know how best to translate its message into our daily lives.

That the Bible speaks to individual life and personal issues, millions of Christians testify. The eternal God lives in its pages and speaks through it with the same power and authority that He did when it was first written. How foolish we are if we fail, then, to study it daily; store precious fragments of it in our memory; learn its highways and byways and make reading it reverently a priority each day.

As 'faith comes from hearing the message, and the message is heard through the word of Christ' (Rom. 10:17. NIV) then it follows that your evangelistic endeavours must be based firmly on God's Word. The better you know the Bible, the more effective you will be in leading people to Jesus Christ.

Remember the thrilling story in Acts chapter 8 of Philip's encounter with the Ethiopian official in

Samaria? While Philip was involved in a tremendous spiritual awakening in Samaria, the Holy Spirit spoke to him and told him to go into the desert. Imagine being picked up from a thrilling revival and being set down in a desert! If it had been me I think I would have said, 'Lord, what's the point of looking for souls in a desert? Let me stay in the exciting atmosphere of Samaria where things are really happening.'

But Philip seemed to accept the change and challenge without equivocation. In fact, we read that when Philip saw the Ethiopian eunuch crossing the desert in his chariot, he ran with great eagerness towards him. He found the traveller reading from part of the Scriptures – the 53rd chapter of Isaiah. Now Philip was well-versed in the Old Testament Scripture. So he began right at the place where the Ethiopian eunuch was reading and 'preached unto him Jesus'.

If you came across someone reading Genesis 1 or Deuteronomy 23 or Esther 4, would you be able to 'Preach unto them Jesus'? To do this requires an understanding of how the Scriptures correlate – their sequential history, their types, their inner meaning.

You see, Jesus is the main message of the Bible. All the Old Testament truths converge on Him; all the New Testament truths emerge from Him. He is the hub of the Scriptures. He is the heart of the Evangel.

To be able to go to any Scripture and lead a person to Christ requires a close study of the Bible as a whole. We communicate to others only from out of our own understanding and our own resources. Learn to spend time, therefore, in the

Scriptures. Study the Bible not only for your own personal pleasure but for the profit of others. Take a correspondence course with one of the Bible colleges, and get to know the Bible so intimately that whatever page you open, you can find a path that leads to Jesus.

Philip had what it took to be an evangelist – he knew the Word of God, and was able to communicate and deliver God's truth in a way that was tremendously effective. Remember this – the more you acquaint yourself with the Bible, the more God can use you. I have seen this principle at work in my own life, and in the lives of countless other Christians. It never fails.

Get close to God in prayer

John Wesley, that great servant of God, gave us a clear cut gauge for testing the reality of our spiritual life. He wrote: 'Do you pray always? Do you rejoice in God every moment? Do you, in everything, give thanks – in loss, in pain, in sickness, in weariness, disappointments? Do you fear nothing? Do you feel the love of God continually in your heart? Have you a witness, in whatever you speak or do, that it is pleasing to God?'

Strong words. They search the life relentlessly, especially the words: 'Do you pray?' There is no way we can build a close relationship with God if we scrap the disciplined practice of prayer. 'The way to know Christ with intimacy,' says one writer, 'is to talk with Him, to talk with Him daily, and to talk for more than a few moments.'

Dr John Stott, the well-known Anglican minister and Rector Emeritus of All Souls, Langham

Place, London, says, 'The thing I know will give me the deepest joy, namely to be alone and unhurried in the presence of God, aware of His presence, my heart open to worship Him, is often the thing I least want to do.'

I can identify with John Stott's statement. And so, I am sure, can you. Most Christians know that to develop their spiritual life they must spend time with God in prayer, yet there is something within them that resists that responsibility.

That is why we must make a daily *appointment* with God – a specific time when we meet with Him – for such an important thing as prayer cannot be left to the vagaries of feeling. If you come to think in terms of having a daily appointment with God, then you are more likely to keep it even when you don't feel like it.

Aim, if you can, to have your prayer time in the morning.

Why the morning? Well, the mind is rested and fresh, und there is a forward-looking aspect to the day. 'Make conscience of beginning the day with God,' said John Bunyan, 'and the best way to begin the day well is to begin it the night before.' Earlier retiring will result in earlier rising.

A regular early morning prayer habit will soon build itself into your life, and will come to have the regularity and naturalness of other daily responsibilities, like washing, eating meals, etc. You should not, of course, limit your praying to that early morning prayer time. You can pray anywhere and at any time – in the street, walking to work, in a bus or train. But let those prayers be extras. Growth in the Christian life demands discipline, and so whatever you do, be firm with yourself about a fixed period of daily prayer.

How should the time in prayer be spent?

Begin by reading a portion of the Scriptures. George Muller, that great saint of a past generation, said that reading the Bible, prior to engaging in prayer, was the greatest discovery he had made in fifty years of discipleship. For the first ten years of his Christian life, it was his custom, after having dressed in the morning, to go straight to prayer. But he found the results disappointing. Then he decided to begin his daily quiet time with a brief reading from the New Testament. Immediately there was a dramatic difference. He said, 'After a few minutes, my soul was led to confession, or to intercession, or to supplication, so that, though I did not, as it were, give myself to *prayer*, but to *meditation* yet it turned almost immediately more or less into prayer.' (*Autobiography of George Muller*, p. 153, Nisbet.)

Reading the Bible, prior to your prayer time, will bring you swiftly into the conscious presence of God. Mind-wandering is largely prevented and prayer is made easy.

Take a notebook and a pencil into your prayer time, and be prepared to write down the name, or names, of those for whom God wants you specially to intercede.

'Before I talk to men about God, I talk to God about men,' said one famous soulwinner. He went on to say that he often found that before he met a person during the day, God had already laid that person's name upon his heart that very morning while in prayer. The intercession he made for that person was, as he put it, the softening-up process, enabling his verbal witness to fall like seed upon prepared ground.

Many years ago I knew a young girl in the north of England who made it a daily practice to ask God for the name of someone for whom she should pray that day, and then follow up with a personal talk on salvation. One morning, to her great consternation, the Lord laid upon her heart the name of her headmaster. At first she was overcome with fear, but as she prayed, the fear dissolved and she set out for school.

On the way, she wondered how the Lord would enable her to have an opportunity to speak to her headmaster about Christ, but upon arriving at school and checking the noticeboard, she found that her name was amongst a list of names of people the headmaster wanted to see that day. The appointment turned out to be on a small matter to do with the school fete, but when it was over she asked if she might talk about something of personal importance. He agreed, so she told him how the Lord had laid his name upon her heart that morning, and then went on to share with him, in a very simple way, a personal testimony to the power and grace of Christ in her life.

The headmaster said little at the time, but later that evening, after staying on to work on some school reports, he bowed his head over his desk and received Jesus Christ as his Lord and Saviour.

Of course, praying for God to give you a name will not always result in such dramatic consequences. Those who practice this approach to evangelism (by asking God for the names of certain individuals for whom they should pray and to whom they should witness) say that it is more a question of sowing than reaping.

Occasionally, however, there are those moments when one sees the hands of God moving in a wonderful way. Three men I read about recently – Luther J. Porter, W. E. Sangster and Cecil Pawson – said that one day God laid upon their hearts the name of a man for whom they should pray. At that time he was a notorious cynic and an agnostic. They prayed for him for years before he became a Christian. And his name? Malcolm Muggeridge!

Open your heart to the Holy Spirit (Acts 1:8)

No one can build a vital relationship with God unless they enter into a day to day dependency upon the Holy Spirit. Paul told the Ephesian Christians to 'be filled with the Spirit' (Eph. 5:18). And he was not referring here to a one-off experience. The tense of the original Greek (as preachers are at pains to point out) is in the present continuous and should be read: 'Be being filled with the Holy Spirit.'

The Amplified New Testament puts it thus: 'And do not get drunk with wine, for that is debauchery, but *ever* be filled and stimulated with the Holy Spirit.'

But this is often where the Christian Church is weakest. It believes in and teaches the Holy Spirit – partly.

A young minister I heard of had a nervous, rundown condition which a private physician diagnosed as followed: 'You are trying to build a £50,000 house with £25,000 resources. You are strained and worried over the inadequate resources. Cost of diagnosis – £25.' That diagnosis could be given to a large number in the contemporary Christian church. We are trying to do things beyond our natural resources – hence strain. We must tap new resources.

The Holy Spirit is in the world in order to provide us with all the resources we need to do God's work in God's way.

Not so long ago, I visited the town of Houston, Texas, and while browsing in a bookshop there, I came across a small booklet entitled *A new level of power*. It told how, in the early years after they had discovered oil in Texas, the supply threatened to run out. One day someone dared to drill deeper than the usual depth of 2,500 feet, and went to a depth of 5,000 feet. Immediately he struck a new level of oil which brought forth one of the strongest gushers they had ever seen in the State. Now almost all the oil is tapped at that level.

When we as Christians go down to the deeper levels and tap the resources available to us in Christ, then we, like the oil wells of Texas, shall be artesian and overflowing.

Roy Swann, a friend of mine, and currently office manager of Crusade for World Revival, was, until he had a dramatic encounter with the Holy Spirit several years ago, one of God's 'frozen people'. All his Christian life he had discharged his responsibilities with great care and concern, but he lacked that vital inner glow which comes from a living contact with the Holy Spirit. In a prayer meeting one night an invitation was given to those who felt they had not experienced the fullness of the Holy Spirit in their lives, to come forward for prayer. Roy responded, and when he was prayed for, he experienced an inner release and an anointing of the Spirit that set his whole being on fire.

Roy's life was transformed from a thermometer to a thermostat – from merely registering the temperature of his surroundings to changing it! He goes around now sharing God's love with people in a way that is truly refreshing, and he says that his encounter with the Holy Spirit was as real and almost as life-changing as his conversion many years previously.

I am aware, of course, that in talking about the subject of being filled with the Holy Spirit, I am treading upon delicate ground. There are those who claim that when we are converted we are filled with the Holy Spirit, and it is then our responsibility to keep the supply of the Spirit 'topped up' in our lives.

Others claim that when we become Christians, we receive Christ into our hearts, but that we need to have a further encounter with the Holy Spirit in order to be effective witnesses for Christ.

Then there are those who say that although the Holy Spirit enters into us at conversion, we need another operation of the Spirit if we are to become effective witnesses for Him. This, they claim, comes only when we open our beings fully to God at some point subsequent to our conversion.

The great danger here is that we can become so bogged down in doctrinal discussion that we miss out on the very thing we most need – the Holy Spirit's personal presence and power.

I am not concerned here about entering into a discussion of the theological implications of what is often called 'the baptism in the Holy Spirit', but let me just ask you a simple question: are you aware of the Holy Spirit's power flowing and pulsing through your life at this very moment? If you are, then fine. I am happy for you. If you are not, then let me urge you to open your heart to God and invite Him to fill you to overflowing by the power of His Spirit.

A little boy, when asked what the Holy Spirit means, replied, 'I suppose it is what puts the 'umph' in Christianity.'

It is! It is also very much more. He puts everything – everything which a Christian needs for effective living – into Christianity. Whatever your doctrinal position, and whatever your views on how the Spirit functions in the life of a Christian, if, in answering the question I asked you a few moments ago, you discovered that there is an emptiness in your life or a lack of divine zeal, then put it right at this moment. Kneel in God's presence and ask Him to fill you (or refill you) with the plenitude of His Spirit. The issue is not so much whether you have the Holy Spirit, but rather, does the Holy Spirit have you?

Link yourself to a live Christian fellowship

Several years ago a whitewashed slogan appeared on the walls of a university which said: 'Humpty Dumpty was pushed!' The person who wrote those words identified a problem with which we are all familiar – we are all 'broken' people. We await the arrival of the 'King's men' to put us together again.

Someone has described the Christian Church as

being filled with 'walking wounded'. The best of us have feelings of deep inadequacy or crippling inability.

Does this mean that we have to wait until we are fully whole before we go out and engage in the task of winning men and women to Jesus Christ?

No. The Almighty sends us out into the world to be salt and light, and even as we go He seasons the salt and trims the wick. A healthy church is a church where the members recognise that they are all Christians in the making and relate to each other as being 'under construction'.

There are many distinguishing marks of a true local church, but one of the most important is its capacity for sharing. In Hebrews 10:24–25 we read: 'And let us consider how we may spur one another on toward love and good deeds. Let us not give up meeting together, as some are in the habit of doing, but let us encourage one another – and all the more as you see the Day approaching' (NIV).

God has made us dependent people – not only dependent upon Him and His resources, but dependent upon each other. There is no room in the Christian Church for the independent only the interdependent. Paul puts it like this: 'One part of the body cannot say to the other part of the body, "I have no need of you" ' (1 Cor. 12:21).

Several years ago, when I was in the United States, I saw a television programme which featured Robert Schuller, the famous pastor of the Crystal Cathedral in Garden Grove, Los Angeles. In an address he gave to an audience of several thousand, he told the story of a man who one night had a remarkable dream.

He saw himself in a large banquet hall where a table was covered with delicious goods of every variety. People were sitting around the table, obviously very eager to tuck in – but there was one problem. Everyone's arms were bound to boards so they were unable to bend their elbows. They managed to reach the food, but couldn't get it into their mouths!

Finally one guest had a bright idea. He picked up a delicious morsel of food, and leaning across the table to the person opposite, placed it in his mouth. The man who had received the food then returned the favour. Soon everyone caught on, and in no time they had all eaten their fill.

What a fantastic message this dream portrays. It is our privilege. as Christians, to feed our brothers and sisters and to be fed by them. Galatians 6:2 says, 'Carry each other's burdens, and in this way you will fulfil the law of Christ' (NIV).

A true Christian fellowship provides the atmosphere in which God's children are nurtured, strengthened and refreshed so that they can go out into the world to share the revolutionary message that Christ is alive and coming again.

Unfortunately, many churches are what Leighton Ford describes as 'exclusive clubs for hothouse saints instead of hospitals for sinners'!

During a Billy Graham Crusade in America, a highly paid prostitute went to a service and was wonderfully converted. She was recommended to a church near her home, and began at once to attend the services and to become involved in the Christian community. A few weeks after her conversion, the woman who had counselled her telephoned the minister to ask if she was going to make it. 'Oh, she'll make it all right,' said the pastor, 'but I'm not sure my church will!' He went on to say that the people in the church, knowing the girl's past, steered clear of her.

What a tragedy!

But what would happen in your church, I wonder, if say, during the coming week twenty or thirty people from different walks of life were converted to Christ, and next Sunday headed for your church? Would it discover an exclusive club or a hospital for sinners?

A true community of God's people fulfils many functions. It is a school where people are trained and equipped for their personal ministry to others. It is a clinic where people who are hurting can come and share their hurts in an atmosphere of acceptance and love, and go away healed. It is an employment bureau where individual gifts and talents are put to proper use.

Is your church like this? If not, don't spend your time criticising and condemning others. Determine to be a model that others can follows. Say to yourself:

If everyone in my church was just like me,
What kind of church would my church be?

If you find yourself in a church where the Bible is not believed, where prayer is not a priority and where the principles of discipleship are not expounded and explained, or practised, then you ought to seriously consider moving your allegiance and finding a church that functions according to New Testament standards.

But whatever you do – stop looking for a perfect

church. As one wag said, 'If you ever find one, don't join it, because you'll ruin it!'

Everyone, however, needs to be surrounded by a community of people who, although imperfect, maintain the vision of the local Body of Christ being the launching pad for thrusting Christians out into the community – out to those who are blind to the glories and the majesty of our Lord Jesus Christ.

7: Understanding needs before applying solutions

'Every person is worth understanding,' says Dr Clyde Narramore, one of the founders of the Christian counselling ministry in the United States. Every effort we make to try to understand people will greatly sharpen the cutting edge of our evangelistic ministry.

This doesn't mean that we have to enrol in a course on psychology or go out and purchase every book we can find on the subject of human behaviour. It does mean, however, that we take some pains to think through and try to understand the reasons why people act and behave the way they do.

One of the secrets of Jesus Christ in His relationship with people was the fact that He understood them. The apostle John says of Him: 'He did not need anyone to tell him what people were like: he understood human nature' (John 2:25, J. B. Phillips). We may not have the same degree of insight into people as our Lord, but drawing upon His resources and wisdom, we can greatly deepen our perception and understanding.

One of the axioms of human behaviour is that everyone has basic needs, and everyone is strongly motivated to have those needs met. In fact, an important question we ought to ask ourselves before attempting to interpret the Gospel to a friend or acquaintance is this: how close am I to this person's *felt* needs?

We know, of course, that a person's greatest need is Christ but before we set out to confront them with this fact, we ought to search sensitively and perceptively for the point in their lives where they feel the deepest need. Once we find it, we can then lead the person from where they are to where they should be.

Jesus did this all the time. He seemed to be sensitive and alert to the felt needs of every person He met. There are no fewer than nineteen private conferences between Christ and individuals in the Gospels, and on each occasion He used a different appeal and a different approach.

When Christ talked to Nicodemus, He said, 'You must be born again' (John 3:7). He never, as far as we know, used that same statement to anyone else. He spoke to the woman at Sychar's well about 'living water'. There is no record of Him ever using that phrase anywhere else when speaking to an individual. When the rich young ruler came to Jesus, the Master didn't say: 'You must be born again,' or 'I can give you living water.' No, sensing that money was this man's god, He confronted him with the need to sell all his possessions. With Zacchaeus, who obviously needed friendship more than anything else, Jesus approached him on that level. 'Zacchaeus, come down immediately. I must stay at your house today' (Luke 19:5, NIV).

In every spiritual *tête-a-tête* that Christ held with

a seeking soul, He seemed to sense where people were, related to them at that level, then led them step by step to an awareness of Himself as the Son of God and the Saviour of the world.

Maslow's five levels of needs

One of the best teaching tools I know that helps us relate to a person's felt needs, is that presented by Abraham Maslow, known as Maslow's hierarchy of basic needs. I have used Maslow's model of basic needs in my book *Marriage – As God Intended* (Kingsway), but here I am looking at it from a different perspective.

Maslow believed that all men and women have basically the same set of needs and attempt to satisfy them in a definite order of importance – beginning at the bottom of the pyramid and moving upward (see illustration overleaf).

Although Maslow was not a Christian, he had remarkable insight into the structure of the human personality, and many Christian psychologists now use his hierarchy of needs to illustrate certain aspects of spiritual truth. The five needs in Maslow's list, starting with the lowest or more basic, are:

1. Physical needs (food, warmth, air, water, etc – the elements necessary to maintain physical life).
2. Safety and security needs (Maslow is referring here to physical security, some reasonable confidence that physical needs will be met tomorrow and in the future).
3. Love and affection needs (the need to feel one is loved for one's own sake).

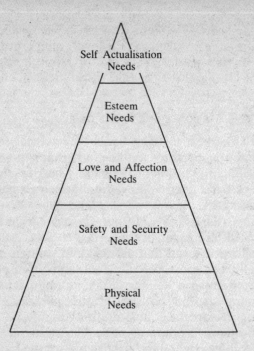

Self Actualisation Needs

Esteem Needs

Love and Affection Needs

Safety and Security Needs

Physical Needs

4. Esteem needs (the need to contribute to one's environment and to make an impact upon one's world).
5. Self-actualisation needs (the need to express oneself to the highest degree of satisfaction, and to become all that one has the potential of becoming).

The main feature in Maslow's theory is that people are not motivated to meet the 'higher' needs until the 'lower or more basic' ones have been met. This means that although all five levels of need are present in an individual, they will not all be operative at the same time.

Physical needs

The most basic needs, of course, are the physical ones. His view is that until these basic needs are largely met then the person is less concerned about the higher needs being met. A person who is starving would hardly be interested in attending a Bible study on the subject 'How to Discover Your Basic Spiritual Gift'! And someone who is worried about how he will find food to sustain himself tomorrow would be unlikely to enrol in a course on the subject of car maintenance.

What does all this mean in practical terms, and in relation to this book? It means, quite simply, that when we share the Gospel, we must seek to relate it to a person's *felt* level of need. If a man is starving then that is hardly the time for a dissertation on the way of salvation as set out in the book of Romans. Someone said that even God can't talk to a starving man except in terms of bread! The great General Booth used to say to his followers, 'When you give a Gospel tract to a hungry man, wrap it up in a sandwich!'

This is why we ought to be grateful for organisations like *Tear Fund* who help feed the hungry and clothe the naked. They interpret the Gospel at the level of a person's *felt* need.

Jesus Himself, before confronting Simon Peter with the challenging question, 'Do you love me?' provided a hot breakfast for the erring disciple (John 21:12). The Master knew that before Simon Peter could respond to such a challenge, his physical needs must first be met.

Over and over again in the Scripture, our Lord reminds us of the importance of ministering to people's physical needs. When done in the right way, the meeting of physical needs is a ministry that will be rewarded in eternity. It is, in fact, a ministry not only done *for* Christ but done *to* Christ. Listen to what Jesus says in these deeply moving verses in Matthew's Gospel:

'Then he will say to those on his left, "Depart from me, you who are cursed, into the eternal fire prepared for the devil and his angels. For I was hungry and you gave me nothing to eat, I was thirsty and you gave me nothing to drink, I was a stranger and you did not invite me in, I needed clothes and you did not clothe me, I was sick and in prison and you did not look after me."

'They also will answer, "Lord, when did we see you hungry or thirsty or a stranger or needing clothes or sick or in prison, and did not help you?"

'He will reply, "I tell you the truth, whatever you did not do for one of the least of these, you did not do for me."

'Then they will go away to eternal punishment, but the righteous to eternal life.' (Matthew 25:41–46, NIV).

Perhaps if we Christians made a more vigorous attempt to minister to people's physical needs, where and when necessary, we might be able more successfully to reach those higher needs.

When a person's physical needs have been largely met, a strange thing happens – they no longer motivate them. A drive that is being met no longer drives. The person is free to focus on

104

higher things. When a person is able to climb above the level of physical needs, a whole set of desires come into play on a higher level.

Safety and security

The second level is the need for safety and security. This involves the need to know that just as today's physical needs have been met, so will tomorrow's. If a person is not reasonably secure that their physical needs will be met tomorrow, then they will not be motivated to think in terms of meeting the higher needs in the hierarchy.

We all need to feel fairly confident that our physical needs will be taken care of tomorrow in the same way that they have been met today. If we feared that tomorrow, and in the days and weeks following, there would be no food in the shops, no water in our taps, no police protection, then doubtless we would feel deeply insecure.

It is my belief that a large proportion of the human race are feeling deprived at this level, particularly as they survey the future and see the way the world is going. Many of the questions uppermost in people's minds are these:

Will law enforcement be able to cope with the growing trend toward violence? Will we see riots and bloody battles on our streets? Will a nuclear war break out and, instead of sending us into eternity in a blinding flash, leave us mutilated and maimed?

Threats like inflation, political unrest, disturbances such as we have seen in some of our inner cities, create a good deal of insecurity in the hearts of some people.

How do we relate to a non-Christian who feels unsure about having his physical needs met in the future? It would be quite pointless, in my view, to try to engage him in a conversation about heaven or the eternal state. What he needs at this level is a realistic and down-to-earth exposition of the Bible truth that God is able to meet the need we have, in order to know that tomorrow our physical needs will be met.

Consider, for example, these clear statements of Scripture:

'Seek ye first the kingdom of God, and his righteousness; and all these things' (referring to food, clothing and shelter) 'shall be added unto you' (Matt. 6:33).

'Take therefore no' (anxious) 'thought for the morrow' (Matt. 6:34).

'Do not be anxious about anything, but in everything . . . present your requests to God . . . my God will meet all your needs according to his glorious riches in Christ Jesus (Phil. 4:6, 19, NIV).

Many people have been drawn to Christ because they see in Him their security for the future. This may be viewed as a selfish motive for coming to Christ, but, when evangelising, people must be accepted for what they are, not as one would like them to be. The task of the evangelist is to lead them from this point to genuine repentance, without which no one can be truly saved or converted.

Love and affection

If a person has their physical and safety needs fairly well met, then their needs on the third level – the need for love and affection – might come to the fore.

The need for love includes the need to belong, to be an appreciated part of a group of human beings. Maslow claims that this is the strongest need in most people today. He may well be right.

This is why a warm, active, loving Christian fellowship will do more to bring people to Jesus Christ than all the evangelistic crusades we can conduct.

I am not saying that we ought to abandon mass evangelism. It is vital that we reach out to people through every means available. What I am saying is that we must realise that people are attracted to people. They long to feel an accepted part of a warm, caring community. Many have never experienced that in their family situation, and when they are introduced to the loving fellowship of the Church, they feel at once that this is where they 'belong'.

I am convinced that bringing people into a loving, caring Christian fellowship is the most powerful form of evangelism. In spite of all its sad failings, the local church is the best instrument that there is for bringing people to Christ. The deep need of a person's heart, at the level of which we are speaking here, ought to be met by simply saying, 'Come and see.'

Bring an unbeliever into a church where love and care are practised, and it will not be long before his incredulity will give way to faith. Let him sample fellowship of the quality described in the New Testament, and something deep inside him will say, 'This is it.'

What a task for the local church – for *every* local church. How sad that the Christian family is often a contradiction of its own family ideal: divided into cliques, lacking in spiritual dynamism, split with internal jealousies, cold, forbidding and exclusive.

Is it any wonder that we are less effective than we might be? It is our plain duty to wipe this reproach from the Christian Church and show the world now that we are the society of God's intention. And when we do, there will be no greater way than meeting a person's need at this level – the need for love.

The Scriptures make it clear that just as God has met our needs on the preceding two levels – physical and safety needs – so He meets our needs on the level of love and affection. Consider such texts as the following:

'Who shall separate us from the love of Christ? Shall trouble or hardship or persecution or famine or nakedness or danger or sword? . . . I am convinced that neither death nor life, neither angels nor demons, neither the present nor the future, nor any powers, neither height nor depth, nor anything else in all creation, will be able to separate us from the love of God that is in Christ Jesus our Lord' (Romans 8:35 38, 39, NIV).
'But God demonstrates his own love for us in this: while we were still sinners, Christ died for us.' (Romans 5:8, NIV).

'This is love: not that we loved God, but tha[t] he loved us and sent his Son as an atoning sacrifice for our sins.' (1 John 4:10, NIV).

Many people have been drawn into the Kingdom of God through experiencing the warmth of a loving, caring Christian fellowship. They have seen among God's people a love that perhaps they never witnessed in their own families. And such a love, when demonstrated in the power of the Holy Spirit, is a love that conquers antipathy and overwhelms all suspicion and distrust.

What if it has been a person's good fortune to surmount these first three levels? Let's assume their physical needs, their safety needs and their need for acceptance and love are fairly adequately met. What's the fourth step on Maslow's pyramid?

Self-worth and self-esteem

It's the need for self-worth and self-esteem. Every person in the world needs to feel they are valuable and important, and they fail to function effectively if there is a weakness in this area.

It was on this level that the message of Christ's Gospel made its appeal to my heart when I was first confronted with it. I suffered from a deep inferiority complex, and although I was brought up in a family where my physical needs, my safety needs and my needs for love and affection were greatly met, I still felt very inferior.

Sermons about Christ's power to meet my physical needs just went over my head. Messages that focused on God's keeping and supplying power in the future made no impression on me.

Even the loving caring Christian fellowship into which I was introduced, made no impact upon my life.

One day, however, a visiting preacher to the Mission Hall I attended, said something that touched my heart deeply. He said that I mattered to God. The Almighty had a purpose for my life which could not be duplicated by any other individual. I was unique. God saw me before I was formed in my mother's womb. I was special to Him. These words illuminated my whole being and set fire to my soul. I almost ran the length of the church that night when the preacher gave the invitation for people to come to the front and receive Christ. When I accepted Christ into my life, repented of my sin, and committed my whole being to Him, I found what the preacher said was perfectly true – I was somebody! The more I thought about the purpose of Christ for my life, the more my inferiority dissolved. The Scriptures which ministered to my need were as follows:

'For to me, to live is Christ and to die is gain' (Phil. 1:21, NIV).

'For we are God's workmanship, created in Christ Jesus to do good works, which God prepared in advance for us to do' (Eph. 2:10, NIV).
'He redeems my life from the pit and crowns me with love and compassion' (Psalm 103:4, NIV).

Does the Gospel have any 'good news' for the

person struggling with the need for self-worth and self-esteem? Thank God, it does.

How did Jesus approach those He encountered who suffered from a negative self-image? He built up that person's self-respect. By going to Zacchaeus' house as his guest, Jesus did something for that man that perhaps nothing else could have achieved. When He met Mary Magdalene, He treated her with such respect, that it transformed her life.

If someone with an immoral reputation invited me to have a meal with him, I might feel a little ashamed to be seen with him. It would injure my dignity. If someone who is my equal invited me to have dinner with him, I would be pleased, but it would hardly boost my self-esteem. If someone much higher up the social scale, say the Queen of England, invited me to have a meal with her, then that would give my self-esteem quite a lift!

Jesus Christ, as you will no doubt readily admit, is higher than the highest of earth's dignitaries. When He came to me, through the words of a humble preacher, now close on forty years ago, and convinced me that He wanted to live His life through me . . . well – I haven't got over it yet!

Of course, I hesitated for a while. There was a moment when I thought I was not good enough for Him. But then He took off His robe of righteousness and put it around me. 'Here, wear this,' He seemed to say. 'This will entitle you to be as accepted in heaven as I am.'

When I accepted Christ, and He came into my life, He gave such a boost to my self-esteem that for the first time in my life I found I was able to accept myself. Real self-esteem began to grow and emerge. I was somebody! And the wonder of that fact has never left me.

Self-actualisation

The fifth and final stage in Maslow's hierarchy of needs is that of self-actualisation. This is an all-embracing term to describe a number of needs and desires – the quest for intellectual understanding, aesthetic enjoyment, creativity, self-expression and so on. According to Maslow, these lie dormant in us because we have not learned how to satisfy the lower needs.

Self-actualisation is the need to realise one's potential by a full development of one's inner capacities. No one can have his psychological and spiritual needs fully satisfied apart from a personal encounter with Jesus Christ. This is why thousands of people who have risen to great heights in life, achieved great standards or done tremendous exploits, suffer from what someone has called destination sickness. They have arrived . . . but empty!

Joseph Alrich says of such people, 'People need a worthwhile purpose which links their achievement to something beyond their own self-interests. They need to know that it is possible to achieve and receive eternal dividends. Many would be delighted to discover that there is the possibility of hearing the Lord of the universe say, "Well done, thou good and faithful servant." Maybe we should tell them.'

Although Maslow's hierarchy of needs must be seen only as a tool, it is extremely helpful in finding or determining the level of need a person is struggling to satisfy. A motivation to act appears to be directly related to a felt need. If I can link the Gospel to a felt need, I create a favourable climate for action. If I am hungry, I am motivated to meet that need. All my thoughts and desires turn to food. If my need for food is extremely strong, then all my other desires become subordinate to that one desire – how can I meet my need?

When relating to non-Christians, you should ask yourself: what need is this person trying to meet? Don't aim too high – they may not even be aware that they have those desires. Don't aim too low, unless it is fairly obvious, because perhaps those lower needs don't drive them anymore. Ask the Holy Spirit to help you discover what the person's need is right now. If you can honestly relate your message to their level of need, then you are on the way to success.

There are those, of course, who will object to this approach, and say it is time-wasting and time-consuming. They prefer to confront people directly with their need of Christ, letting the chips fly where they will. This may be a valid approach at certain times and with certain individuals, but generally it is better by far to find the point where a person senses a deep deprivation in their being and speak to that need with the help and aid of the Holy Spirit.

George Hunter in his book *The Contagious Congregation* suggests an interesting refinement of

Maslow's hierarchy, when using it for evangelistic purposes. He says that people who are driven by needs in the top two sections of the pyramid are the stronger, more adequate, people. Those at the bottom are the weaker, more vulnerable ones.

People at the top are more self-sufficient, independent and relatively strong. People near the bottom of the hierarchy (the first three levels of needs) are more dependent and relatively weak personalities.

An important evangelistic key for those who are at the top of the pyramid, is the revelation that God has a purpose for their lives. For those at the bottom, the evangelistic key is the demonstration by your deeds as well as by your words, that you really do care.

Over the centuries, the Christian Church has found that its evangelistic efforts are more effective amongst what we used to call the down and outs. These are the people struggling with hunger, safety and security needs. The ministries of the Church, such as caring for the poor, relief work and so on, are very effective with those who are more aware of their needs on the first three levels.

The day has come, I believe, when we must focus on the higher needs, especially here in the West where physical and safety needs are not as predominant as in the Third World.

The Christian's task in witnessing is to find out where a person is on the hierarchy of needs and to engage them at that level.

Someone said that to evangelise the weak people, we must find a need and show them that we care. To evangelise the strong, we involve them in discovering God's highest purpose for their lives.

Summary

A crucial question to ask yourself when interpreting the Gospel to your friends and acquaintances, then, is: how close am I to this person's felt needs? You may witness to them eloquently about heaven, but if, at that moment, they are struggling with the problem of unemployment, then your words will not relate to their *felt* need. You have to find the level on which a person is feeling deprived, lock into that, and minister to them in the strength and power of the Holy Spirit.

A sign painted on the side of a Greyhound bus in the USA says: 'When you deal in basic needs you're always needed.' Once you have discovered how to lock into basic needs, you and the world will never be the same again.

8: Almost persuaded – how hard do we press?

'Evangelism,' said someone, is not just a commission, but a co-mission.' In other words, God and man team up in order to bring souls into the Kingdom. We can't do it without Him, and He won't do it without us.

There are times, of course, when a person appears to come to faith in Christ without any human assistance or intervention. I have no doubt that God is well able to lead people to Himself without human aid. I am simply saying that His *usual* way of enlisting people in His cause is through a combination of human and divine abilities. Christmas Evans, a famous Welsh preacher of centuries ago, used to say that 'almost every soul that enters the kingdom of God has, if you look carefully enough, a human thumb print on it.'

To grasp the fact that bringing people into the Kingdom of God is a matter of teamwork – God and man working together – is to relieve us of a good deal of strain. It also frees us from pride, a fear of failure and arrogance. What is more, it lifts us above the possibility of manipulating people in a dishonest way so that we can get 'results'.

Many years ago I was present at a seminar on Evangelism, at which one of the instructors made the remark: 'I don't care what method you use as long as it brings people to Jesus Christ. If it works and produces a person's conversion, then go ahead and do it, whatever it is.'

To him the end justified the means. He was, I know, echoing the feelings of many Christians who assume that any method of witnessing is good as long as it brings results. I wish to challenge that assumption.

In sharing the faith, our task is to combine a sense of the urgency of the message with a respect for the dignity and rights of people. If the Gospel is 'Good News', then not to share it is criminal. We have no right to keep it to ourselves, but neither do we have any right to press Christian claims upon people to the point of manipulation.

Jesus never manipulated anyone. He longed for their salvation, and earnestly pleaded with them to accept His claims, but He never coerced or forced anyone to respond. Remember the story of the rich young ruler? Jesus loved that young man deeply. He saw in him some fine qualities and coveted him for the Kingdom. Yet, after He had presented to him the way of salvation, and the young man had failed to respond, the Scripture says: 'Jesus watched him go' (Mark 10:23, TLB).

Christ did not race after him and plead with him to give the matter further consideration. Neither did He beg, cajole or add psychological pressure. Having made clear His claims to the rich young ruler, He respected him enough to let him go. The Master knew the difference between persuasion and manipulation. And so must we, if we are to be His disciples.

The ethics of persuasion

Many Christians find it difficult to draw the line between persuasion and manipulation. The tension between a conviction to share the faith and respect for the rights of others can cause a real problem. Let's see if we can think this through in an attempt to resolve the matter.

Persuasion, of course, is perfectly proper and legitimate, providing it functions within proper moral and ethical guidelines. When persuasion moves beyond these guidelines and becomes manipulation then it is wrong.

It becomes obvious that we need to define clearly the difference between persuasion and manipulation, so let's lay down a working definition. Persuasion is the attempt we make to convince others that our convictions are true and worthy of acceptance. Manipulation is an attempt to persuade others in a way that restricts their freedom to reject our appeal.

In Acts 26 we read a detailed account of Paul's defence before King Agrippa. The king was greatly impressed with Paul's reasoning concerning the Christian faith, and said, 'Almost you persuade me to be a Christian' (Acts 26:28). Why wasn't Agrippa fully persuaded to become a Christian? Was it that the apostle Paul's preaching did not come up to standard? Did the Holy Spirit fail to do His work properly on that occasion? No. All that was necessary to share Christ was done, and Paul, recognising that his attempts to persuade were not successful, respected the rights of the king too much to add further pressure.

We must do all we can to bring people to Christ, but there is a point where we must hold back, for any attempt to persuade someone to accept salvation in a way that restricts their freedom to choose for or against Christ is wrong.

God has a good deal to say in the Scriptures about the ethics of persuasion. The whole of the second chapter of 1 Thessalonians bears down upon this point:

'So you can see that we were not preaching with any false motives or evil purposes in mind; we were perfectly straightforward and sincere. For we speak as messengers from God, trusted by him to tell the truth; we change his message not one bit to suit the taste of those who hear it; for we serve God alone, who examines our hearts' deepest thoughts. Never once did we try to win you with flattery, as you very well know, and God knows we were not just pretending to be your friends so that you would give us money! As for praise, we have never asked for it from you or anyone else, although as apostles of Christ we certainly had a right to some honour from you. But we were as gentle among you as a mother feeding and caring for her own children. We loved you dearly – so dearly that we gave you not only God's message, but our own lives too' (1 Thess. 2:3–8, TLB).

A similar theme is presented by the apostle in his letter to the Corinthians.

'We have set our faces against all shameful secret practices; we use no clever tricks, no dishonest manipulation of the Word of God. We speak the plain truth and so commend ourselves to every man's conscience in the sight of God. If our gospel is 'veiled', the veil must be in the minds of those who are spiritually dying. The god of this world has blinded the minds of those who do not believe, and prevents the light of the glorious gospel of Christ, the image of God, from shining on them. For it is Christ Jesus as Lord whom we preach, not ourselves; we are your servants for Jesus' sake. God, who first ordered light to shine in darkness, has flooded our hearts with his light, so that we can enlighten men with the knowledge of the glory of God, as we see it in the face of Christ. This priceless treasure we hold, so to speak, in common earthenware – to show that the splendid power of it belongs to God and not to us' (2 Cor. 4:2–7, J. B. Phillips).

A good illustration of taking persuasion beyond its proper limits, is the tactics used by the group known as Jehovah's Witnesses.

Ever been visited by one?

Let me say right away that I am tremendously impressed by their zeal and enthusiasm, but there is something about their mood and manner that puts me right off. Whenever I speak to them, I sense that they are not interested in me as a person, but simply in winning me to their cause. They have pre-planned answers to every question, and if they don't know the answer, they go off and do some research, then come back a few nights later with the answer all neatly tied up.

I have spent endless hours talking to them, and the way they use a relentless procession of proof texts leaves me cold. I get the feeling that they set out, not to convince and persuade, but to manipulate me into their way of thinking. And I resent being manipulated – as I'm sure you do too. The Jehovah's Witnesses attract certain types to their organisation, particularly those who are awed by argument; but I am afraid that in their efforts to make converts, they show very little respect for individual autonomy.

Love and justice

Christian thinkers have usually identified two main elements in persuasion – love and justice. 'Love,' said Charles Finney, 'is the bringing about of the highest good in the life of another person.' The loving persuader wants to bring as many as he can into the Kingdom of God. Justice is concerned with universal obligations – the rights and wrongs of life. The just persuader will care about the rightness and wrongness of his attempts to influence. Such questions as: 'Is it ever right to lie?' or 'Is it wrong to play on people's emotions?' are questions of justice.

Some Christians are loving but not just. Others are just but not loving. The secret is to have these qualities perfectly balanced in one's heart.

Often we attempt to control people when witnessing to them without even realising we are doing it. Are you a manipulating type? To see if you fit into this category, answer these questions:

121

a. Whenever I go out for a meal with my family or a group, do we end up going to the restaurant I prefer? YES/NO

b. Do I enjoy correcting factual errors in people's conversations YES/NO

c. Do I use humour or sarcasm to put people down when I think they are being pompous or arrogant? YES/NO

d. Do I have to know more about a subject than others to feel comfortable discussing it? YES/NO

e. Do I quietly sulk when I am blocked or thwarted in any way? YES/NO

f. Do I react nervously when another person rejects my witness? YES/NO

g. Do I use books, tracts or pamphlets like spiritual 'whips' in a 'You'd-better-read-this-or-else-approach?' YES/NO

h. Can I recognise the times when I ought to keep quiet? YES/NO

i. Do I find myself thinking that the end justifies the means? YES/NO

If your answers are mostly YES then it may be that you are an insecure person. Strange as it may seem, the person who always looks as if they are in command may be the least secure. How secure are you in Christ?

Let's consider now some of the ways or methods of witnessing which border on manipulation.

We are in danger of manipulating people when we see them simply as souls to be won and have lost sight of their rights as persons.

There are some Christians who are more concerned about getting another spiritual 'scalp' than they are for the welfare of the ones to whom they witness. And this is not just a problem in individual witness; it is a problem in mass evangelism too.

During the 1974 Lausanne Congress on World Evangelisation, the point was made that evangelicals have 'become unduly preoccupied with statistics'. The emphasis in some circles seems to be more on success than on the people whom Christ has called us to serve.

In his book *I and Thou*, Martin Buber stresses the immorality of treating a person as merely a means to an end – a thing or an it. He says, 'We must love people and use things, not love things and use people.' He reminds us also that it is not enough just to love God; we must love others as well. If Christians see others simply as things to be used or manipulated, then they will see God in the same way.

The apostle John in his epistle puts it this way:

'Anyone who hates his brother is a murderer, and you know that no murderer has eternal life in him' (1 John 3:15, NIV).

'If anyone says, "I love God," yet hates his brother, he is a liar. For anyone who does not love his brother, whom he has seen, cannot love

123

God, whom he has not seen . . . whoever loves God must also love his brother' (1 John 4:20–21, NIV).

An evangelist I know claims that, when witnessing, he 'never takes no for an answer'. I admire his zeal and his positive approach to witnessing, but I also happen to know that many of his 'converts' say yes simply to get away from him. Persuasion means giving people the right to say no.

Not so long ago, my wife and I were flying from Miami to Dallas, and in the seat in front of us was a Christian businessman, who, as soon as he sat down, turned to the person sitting next to him and said, 'Excuse me, sir, are you interested in spiritual things?'

The man appeared somewhat nonplussed and replied: 'Well . . . er . . . no, not really.'

Undeterred by this, the Christian, hardly drawing a breath, went into a thirty-minute spiel which ended with the statement: 'Now what are you going to do – accept or reject Christ?'

The man to whom the Christian was witnessing was doing his best to be polite, but at that stage, he excused himself and went to the toilet. When he came out, he moved down the plane and found himself another seat.

I applaud every effort made by God's people to witness to the saving power of Jesus Christ; but love for souls must always be balanced by justice. God doesn't gatecrash His way into men's and women's hearts. Why should we?

*We are in danger of manipulating people when we
fail to 'tell it as it really is'.*

One form of witnessing, used I am sad to say
by a great number of Christians, is the 'come to
Jesus and you'll never have any problems again'
approach. Actually it is a form of spiritual seduc-
tion. It is only presenting part of the truth.

Some years ago, when I was a pastor of a church
in central London, I organised a weekly evangelistic outreach into the heart of Soho. All who were
involved in that outreach used to meet in the
centre of Soho, hold a five-minute prayer meeting
in the street, and then split up into two's to mingle
with the crowds and make contact with those who
were willing to listen to the Christian message.
My task was to supervise the operation, and so,
remaining at a discreet distance, I would listen in
on conversations and assist if necessary or advise
on a different approach.

One night I heard one of the young people say,
'If you come to Christ you will never have another
problem. He will solve all your difficulties, find
you a job, enable you to make enough money to
keep yourself, and make you a successful person.'

I took her aside afterwards and gently told her
that her appeal was one-sided and presented an
incomplete picture of the Christian life. 'But,' she
said, 'I wanted her to come to Christ so much that
I felt that if I told her the whole truth it would
put a damper on her response.'

I could understand the girl taking that line in
her witness, but I am also glad to say that when

the matter was pointed out to her, she never, as far as I know, did it again.

The Gospel does not promise that if we come to Christ, we will have money, success or a better job. It does promise, of course, that with Christ in our lives we have the potential for overcoming all our difficulties. But the Christian life is not just, as someone described it, 'a happy hour, every hour'. There are times when the going is tough, and when it means doing things you don't feel like doing. This is a side to Christianity which is not often referred to in Christian witnessing, and by avoiding it we diminish the Gospel.

It is my experience that people tend to be more responsive when the two aspects of the Gospel are presented – the challenges as well as the changes. We must be careful that we don't put the 'happiness' side of the Gospel in bold letters and the demands of discipleship in small print.

Laying on guilt

We are in danger of manipulating people when we attempt to make them feel guilty.

There is a great deal of difference between guilt produced by the Holy Spirit and guilt produced by human pressure. Of course, guilt is a very powerful motivator. Guilt can produce immediate outward response to our urging for Christian commitment. However, guilt that is produced psychologically, and is not the direct result of the Holy Spirit's work, can result in a distorted view of God, and a desire to avoid Him.

We can load guilt on to people when we tell them such things as:

'God won't love you unless you receive Christ.'
'How do you think God feels when you keep
pushing Him away from you like this?'

There is an interesting story about a boy who
wouldn't eat his prunes after dinner. His mother
said, 'God won't like you if you don't eat them.'
He continued to resist until finally she sent him
to his room. A few minutes later a severe thunder-
storm broke out, so his mother tiptoed into his
room to see if he was all right. She found her little
boy saying out loud, 'God, why do you have to
make such a fuss over a few lousy prunes?'
Perhaps conviction of sin is best left to the Holy
Spirit.

A couple of psychologists, J. M. Carlsmith and
A. E. Gross, writing in the volume *Journal of
Personality and Social Psychology* (USA) state
that using guilt to motivate people has adverse
effects. One of the effects is that of avoidance.
When someone makes us feel guilty, we do everything we can to avoid them in the future. Another
effect is devaluation. We tend not to like or
respect those who increase our guilt.

Of course, the question will be raised: 'But
shouldn't people be made to feel guilty for rejec-
ting Christ, and turning their back upon God?'
Most decidedly yes. But the guilt they feel should
come from conviction of sin by the Holy Spirit
and not be the result of human manipulation. Paul
draws the distinction when he writes:

'For God sometimes uses sorrow in our lives to
help us turn away from sin and seek eternal
life. We should never regret his sending it. But

127

the sorrow of the man who is not a Christian is not the sorrow of true repentance and does not prevent eternal death' (2 Cor. 7:10, TLB).

As Christ's ambassadors, it is our responsibility to make ourselves available to God, to interpret His word to people and to share with them the truths of the Gospel. But we must never try to convict people of sin. That is the sacred work of the Holy Spirit.

The Gospel 'Trap'

We are in danger of manipulating people when we try to 'trap' them into listening to or giving their attention to a Gospel presentation.

Nyla Whitmore in her book *How to Reach the Ones You Love* tells how at one period in her life she set about trying to manipulate her husband Jerry into accepting Christ. After she had witnessed to him of her conversion, he seemed to show little interest, so she came up with the idea of what she calls 'household plants' – Bibles, books, tracts and pamphlets. She says,

'If I couldn't convince him with my own words, I'd use those of others to assure him I was no weirdo. I "planted" our library with underlined Bibles, books with notes scrawled in the margins and an occasional tract. Sometimes I'd set a book at an angle and later go back to see if it had been moved. I was always quoting Bible verses, but Bible verses were never meant to be used as spiritual whips to flog our listeners.'

Nyla goes on to say in her book that the way she eventually won her husband to Christ was by taking off the human pressure and responding to him as a dutiful and loving wife.

I know scores of women, who, having failed to see their husbands respond to the Gospel by strong manipulation, have seen them won to Christ when they took off the evangelistic pressure and related to them as a wife and not an evangelist. Some Christians tend to hurl the Gospel at their unconverted husband or wife (as well as others) without a thought for their humanity.

I believe God wants us to be 'up front' with people when we feel it right to share with them the truths of the Gospel. We should make them aware of what we want to share, and be assured of their willingness to listen before we embark on our presentation.

How many of us have been guilty of inviting a non-Christian to an evangelistic event without telling them what is going to happen? Usually at some point in the proceedings a high-powered evangelist unloads both barrels and the 'guest', having no idea of the function or purpose of the invitation, feels trapped and embarrassed.

If you want to invite a friend or an acquaintance to an event where you know the Gospel will be presented, then explain to them what will happen. Say something like this: 'I'd like you to come with me to a Christian event which is designed for Christians and non-Christians. There will be singing, some music, and a speaker will explain and interpret some of the facts relating to Christianity. If at any point you feel you would like to leave, then just give me a nudge and I'll leave with you.' If you prepare a person for what will happen then you are, in my view, doing as Paul said, sharing the Gospel without any dishonest tricks or manipulation.

'Canned' techniques

We are in danger of manipulating people when we attempt to fit them into a pre-planned approach or a 'canned' technique.

Let me be quite clear about what I am saying here. I am not saying it is unhelpful to have in mind an outline of the steps of salvation such as the Four Spiritual Laws or the approach mentioned in *Evangelism Explosion*. Such outlines, which move systematically from man's sin to God's salvation, can be extremely useful when leading a person to Christ; but there can be dangers and limitations.

First, people can sense when you are trying to fit them into a 'canned' approach. Second, no technique will work with everyone. And third, it can depersonalise one's witnessing.

Far too much witnessing follows the sales technique principle. Evangelism is more than a sales technique. If we are to be like Jesus then we must treat others as persons not clients.

When I was a young Christian, I was invited to counsel in an evangelistic crusade being held in one of the towns in the Welsh valleys. My training had consisted of learning by rote a simple formula that was called 'The Way of Salvation'. The idea was that following the appeal in the large crusade service, people would be invited to the front where they would meet a 'counsellor' who would take them to a private room, reserved for the purpose, and there lead them through the steps of salvation.

Almost anyone with a moderate degree of affability could have been a counsellor in that crusade. All that was required was to fit the enquirer into the plan, and it all came out right in the end. The text used was; 'Whosoever shall call on the name of the Lord shall be saved' (Acts 2:21). All the counsellor was expected to do was to win the acquiescence of the enquirer, that he did believe on the Lord Jesus Christ. That agreed, the major premise was established. The conclusion was then swiftly and triumphantly drawn: 'Now you are saved.'

No interest was shown in the enquirer as a person; no building up of a relationship. None of the difficulties which the person might have had – intellectual or emotional – were faced. The process of salvation was so stereotyped by this method that it seemed to iron out all the differences of personality and all the varieties of individual need.

Many people passed through 'The Way of Salvation' and found themselves no different than they had been before. I am reminded of the devout 'drunk', referred to by Dr W. E. Sangster in his book *Let me commend*, who had been to the front seven times in a certain crusade, and thanked God that he had been converted every time!

A systematic or methodical approach to sharing the faith can be extremely helpful, as I have said. I don't think I would have got very far in my own witnessing attempts had I not memorised a simple structure that helped me to show people the way of salvation. However, as I grew in experience, I found that I was able to spell out the way of salvation without recourse to a pre-planned technique. Each presentation was tailor-made to suit the individual and occasion.

But perhaps the greatest danger of a 'canned' technique is that we might put more trust in that than we do in God. Paul said to the Corinthians, 'I came to you in weakness and fear, and with much trembling. My message and my preaching were not with wise and persuasive words, but with a demonstration of the Spirit's power' (1 Cor. 2:3–4, NIV). Techniques have their place. Be sure to see them in that light.

As I look back over my life, I realise that there have been many occasions in the past when I have unwittingly tried to manipulate people into the Kingdom of God rather than persuade them. And there have been times when God has used my witness to further His will, and people have surrendered their lives to Jesus Christ.

I'm so glad that I know He has forgiven me for my errors; and He will forgive you too. Knowing that God can work through our failures and mistakes is no excuse, however, for continuing to pursue a method that does not have the proper balance between love and justice.

Remember, people are human beings, not just souls to be won!

9: How to handle resistance

However persuasive we may be as Christ's ambassadors, there will be times when people will openly and positively resist our attempts to win them to Jesus Christ. This resistance can take many forms. It can vary from mild opposition to downright hostility.

How should we deal with resistance? Remembering what we said in the previous chapter about the danger of manipulation, ought we to withdraw whenever we see signs of resistance? Or should we press on and attempt to overcome them?

It ought to be quite clear by now that when a person expressly asks us to discontinue a conversation which bears on the matter of their eternal salvation, or forbids us to engage them any further on that subject, we ought, out of respect for that person, to comply with their request.

Most resistance, however, is not of this type. It usually takes the form of quiet argument or prevarication. If a person does not expressly ask you to discontinue, then, however much they resist, and *providing you are not entering the area of manipulation*, I believe it proper and legitimate to continue to persuade and, if appropriate to invite them to make a decision for Jesus Christ.

As Christian persuaders we should never be

afraid of resistance. Those who have examined the psychology of resistance say that the more strongly a person resists, the deeper their commitment will be when they are finally persuaded.

Dr Jesse Nirenberg in his book *Getting through to people* says that 'in order to persuade someone to your way of thinking or believing, it is necessary that he first pass through a stage of resistance. This resistance arises from his having to give up the position he already has.'

Why do people resist?

There are many theories as to precisely why people resist new concepts and new ideas. Let's examine a few of these to see if they will be helpful to us in our attempts to understand what goes on in the life of a non-Christian when they are confronted with the Gospel.

One theory says that when a person takes on board new ideas or new concepts, this requires a readjustment of a number of other ideas which they hold in their mind. The new thinking has to be made to fit into their associated thinking. And pressure on a person to change is bound to arouse some resistance.

Another theory says that when a person responds to new ideas, a part of what is being said may make sense, but a part of him (the part that has lived fairly comfortably with past ideas) wants to stay in the status quo. The resistance put up is an attempt to argue against the new concepts precisely because they are convincing. If this theory is true, then some types of resistance ought to be seen as a sign that the non-Christian is fully involved in considering your position. He is responding to your arguments even though the response at the moment is expressed in opposing terms. This is because one part of him is in conflict with the other.

Yet another theory claims that the reason why people resist the introduction of new ideas is due to psychological reaction. It states, quite simply, that we have a special desire for that which is removed from our reach. If another person is about to take away some of our options in life, then we automatically react to deter them. The alternatives that are about to be taken away suddenly take on a new interest, and so we will try to re-establish our right to them.

A faculty member in a college tells how, although he was given a pass to have two free lunches a week in the dining hall, he preferred to give it up in favour of some physical exercise. When it was announced that, due to economic problems, the free lunches were to be discontinued, he found himself reacting against the possible loss of benefits, and took steps, along with others to 're-establish his rights'. He now eats in the dining hall regularly twice a week.

Many people regard any effort at persuasion as an attempt to fence them in. They feel it is an impingement on their freedom and thus they react negatively towards the person who tries to proscribe their actions or beliefs. The harder people push, the harder some resist.

The fourth and final theory we shall examine is one that I find particularly intriguing as I have observed it happening myself in the hearts of non-

Christians who are about to make a decision for Jesus Christ.

The theory states that many people are frequently in conflict with themselves through desiring mutually exclusive things – for example, wanting to hold on to their former lifestyle and at the same time wanting Christ. The desire to move in two different directions at the same time produces strong feelings of anxiety. Moving toward either goal means giving up the other. At the same time, one can't remain immobile for that means giving up both goals.

A start is made by the person in the direction of receiving Christ, and as movement in this direction continues, the opposite goal becomes more distant and anxiety rises over giving it up. If the individual mentally backtracks and moves toward the first goal (the non-Christian lifestyle), he encounters again a certain amount of anxiety as the first goal recedes. The result is anxious indecision. Nothing is accomplished, and the person remains in a state of high anxiety until the matter is resolved.

Now suppose you are trying to persuade someone in this condition to receive Christ, and your arguments and presentation appeal to them. Anxiety might arise because you are applying gentle persuasive pressure in one direction, and anxiety mounts as they feel themselves moving away from the opposite goal. Don't be surprised, therefore, if the person mentally digs their heels in and pulls back from you.

It is not unusual for a person in this position to defend against these feelings of anxiety by engaging in vehement opposition. Their voice may become louder, their speech quicker and they may advance new and stronger arguments for maintaining their non-Christian lifestyle.

Now when that happens, here's what you should do – gently ease off the pressure. When opposition is intense, indicating high anxiety or conflict within the person's heart, it is pointless to apply counter-arguments with greater or equal force, since this only makes the other person maintain a strong position in order to keep the conflict unresolved. You see, moving away from either position is too threatening for them.

Abandoning pressure (of argument) causes the other person to abandon their counter-pressure, and will place them in an anxious state again. But don't be over-concerned about this. Remember, the Holy Spirit is also active in the situation, and He will be working with you and through you to try to gain that person's commitment. Actually, any pressure of argument you place on a person in this position will temporarily relieve their anxiety, since, instead of arguing with themselves, which is anxiety-producing, they can now argue with you.

Once you ease off the pressure, the individual concerned has to take over both positions again, for and against; and is back debating with himself. This means that the arguments you presented previously, which you had taken up and abandoned, are claiming their attention once again. At this stage, gently, very gently, recapitulate the arguments you presented previously. At the same time, pray that the Holy Spirit will help the person resolve their inner anxiety by coming to a firm decision to commit themselves to Christ. If you follow this procedure when witnessing to someone whom you sense has a high degree of anxiety, and who is resisting for this reason, then it is highly possible that your tact and gentleness, together with the Holy Spirit's power, will draw them over the line to Christ.

Four signs of resistance

Vehemence, as we have seen, is a sign of resistance. When a person opposes an idea with more intensity than the situation warrants, it suggests that they are not quite comfortable in the position they hold. As we described, they might be in conflict, wanting to move in both directions at once.

Of course, vehemence *could* be the discharge of anger from another source. They may have been previously deeply hurt by a Christian who did not know how to witness supportively, or it may be that they were let down by someone who professed to be a follower of Christ. But, in any case, vehemence probably represents an internal conflict that has not been resolved.

Another sign that a person is resisting is *when they refuse to consider the strength of your arguments*. When this happens, it usually indicates that a person wishes to hold on to their position for reasons which they do not reveal in the discussion. They aren't open to new ideas and concepts, and want to preserve their position because it serves some private need.

A further sign of resistance is *the introduction of irrelevant arguments into the discussion*. When this happens it implies that the person is unable to find any relevant arguments (otherwise, we must assume, they would be used), and the individual concerned is really advancing these arguments as substitutes for real ones.

You will be able to understand people much more easily if you keep in mind that they usually act in the direction of the strongest reason in their hearts or minds. When they give weak reasons, it is because they don't want to reveal the true reasons. Irrelevant arguments are a sign that there is present in the person's mind a hidden irrational basis for opposition.

Jumping from one objection to another at great speed, without giving much attention to the counter-arguments, is another form of resistance. If an objection were really important to such a person, then they would listen carefully to the counter-argument. They would dwell on it, and try to grasp it firmly. You can generally deduce when a person jumps from one objection to another, even after you have presented a strong counter-argument, that the first one didn't mean very much to them. They probably didn't care too deeply about it, otherwise they would probably have stayed with it for a while in an effort to see if it resolved their problem.

The question must now be faced: how do we handle a person who is unwilling seriously to consider and rationally evaluate the claims of Jesus Christ?

Let me present a simple digest of rules which you can apply at once when next confronted with irrational or unreasonable resistance.

'The punishment of irrationality,' said someone, 'is to be the person who is irrational.' In other words, an irrational person is his own worst enemy. Actually irrationality is difficult to face. It's pretty frightening. It touches off, deep inside us, such things as guilt, fear and, as we saw, anxiety. This is why people who are irrational adopt a defence mechanism called 'intellectualisation'. This is an attempt to divert attention and statements. So show sympathetic understanding for the way the person feels.

Now it is important that you understand this, and what is more that you accept the person as he is. When you show a willingness to face irrationality with understanding and acceptance, the person who is engaging in this type of behaviour or response will be less likely to adopt it. The way will be made easier for them to give it up when they see that you accept sympathetically the very irrationality they are trying to hide. This must not be merely a technique – you really must understand the other person's position.

Acceptance of a person, as we said in a previous chapter, does not necessarily mean that you accept the other person's viewpoint, or, indeed, his behaviour. It simply means that you understand the way he feels and the way he thinks.

Another thing that happens when you express understanding of a person's position, is that it encourages him to consider sympathetically your own views and position. Expressing understanding and acceptance encourages the person to reciprocate, to co-operate and look more sympathetically at the points you are making.

Point out to the person that he is resisting

Sometimes a person may resist without knowing that this is what they are doing. In order to focus a person's attention on their own resistance, and do so gently, the Christian might say something like:

'You don't seem to be willing to consider the arguments I have presented. I'm wondering if there is something going on in your feelings that is making it difficult for you to accept the truth of what I am saying.'

It's hard for a person to take offence at a statement that shows sensitivity and concern for their feelings. At the same time the Christian draws the non-Christian's attention to what is happening inside him.

Of course, a person may deny that he is resisting and become entrenched in his resistance, but *identified resistance is harder to maintain than unidentified resistance*. The strength of unreasonable or irrational resistance is that a person does not admit to himself that he is resisting.

Another thing you could say to someone who is resisting is this:

'Whenever I bring up the subject of making a commitment to Christ, you seem to want to return to issues that we dealt with some time ago. I get the feeling that you want to avoid

141

coming to a decision, and you are working hard to avoid being pinned down to actually doing something about it.'

Evaluate the other person's objections
step by step

Many Christians are afraid to pursue a close examination of an objection, and this is where their ability to deal with opposition comes to a halt. So often, rather than coming to grips with an objection, they withdraw or skim right over the surface of it.

I heard one evangelist say that he never dwelt on a person's objections, because if he did then it was likely that the objections would grow larger. Nonsense! Actually the very opposite takes place. Through discussion, the emotional elements are discharged and the objection is reduced to its proper proportions.

We are now bordering on the area of intellectual argument (something I accept, not every Christian can do effectively). It must be said, however that no matter how sound your arguments may be, they can't have a decisive effect until they are placed alongside the other person's objections. Then, and only then, can it be seen which has the greater weight. And it goes without saying that you can't place them alongside one another until you clearly define and comprehend the other person's arguments.

If they don't make their objections clear, then you must guide them towards this before you can ask for a conclusion based on your argument. So many Christians fail in their influence because, instead of exploring the person's objections, they keep repeating their own arguments and ideas.

For example, suppose you have presented the importance of settling one's eternal destiny before departure from his life, and the one to whom you are witnessing demurs on the grounds that they are not ready to make such a momentous decision. Rather than emphasise again the importance of the decision, it would be much better to explore, at this point, just why they are not ready to make a commitment. As you enter into discussion about the reason why they are not ready you might find that the problem is less difficult than it first appeared to be.

It is important to remember that resistance is often based on both rational and irrational elements. Brought into the light of open discussion, the rational elements will remain and can be identified and dealt with. But the irrational elements, similarly exposed, will dissolve of their own accord.

Summary

Dealing with resistance is such an important matter that I feel it necessary to summarise what I have said in order that the previous points may nestle permanently in your mind.

When confronted by opposition or resistance, begin by expressing your understanding of the way a person feels. Say, 'I understand how you feel about the issue and that you . . .' (then paraphrase their objections).

For example, you could say, 'I hear what you

say, Bill, that you feel you are not ready to make a decision for Christ at this time. I appreciate your viewpoint on the matter, and I think I know how you feel for I've been there myself.' (If this is so, of course!)

This should then be followed by a progressive drawing out and clarifying of the resistance. You could say something like this: 'Help me understand, Bill, what is going on in your feelings when you say you are not ready to make this decision. Is it fear that you might not be able to keep it up? Is it a difficulty we have not yet discussed? Can you clarify it a little more for me?'

If a person during the course of discussion, suddenly becomes vehement in their resistance, then withdraw the pressure and be objective.

At some point it may be necessary to make them aware that they are resisting. Don't be afraid to do this, for it is truly a technique of persuasion, not manipulation. Keep in mind what we have said that identified resistance is harder to maintain than unidentified resistance.

In the case of objection-hopping, where a person jumps to another objection before you have hardly had time to answer the previous one, it means that they haven't really presented the most important one. After dealing with a few of the objections, rather than continue to chase them around, it would be better to draw their attention to the fact that they appear to be evading the issues.

You could say, 'Bill, I realise the objections you have brought up are important, and need to be answered, but I get the feeling that there is still something more important bothering you.'

144

When serious objections are presented, then evaluate them one by one. If you can't answer them at that point, then say so, and try to arrange another time, after you have had time to think through the objections and come up with clear answers for them.

What if after pursuing the techniques of friendly persuasion, the person still doggedly resists? If after expressing understanding, identifying resistance and evaluating the person's objections, they still firmly resist, then terminate the discussion. But do it lovingly, gently, and with great concern. Let there be tears in your heart if not in your eyes. To bring it to a conclusion rather than continuing interminably is the most loving thing to do. Commit the person to God prayerfully in your heart, and keep in mind that, though your ways part, the Holy Spirit will still continue to use what you have said in the days and weeks that lie ahead.

The process of resisting is common to us all. The child resists the discipline of its parents. The student resists the demands of the teacher. The teenager resists the requests of friends. The employee resists the direction of the employer. Husbands resist their wives and wives resist their husbands. For some people, resistance is a way of life.

Resistance can be narrowed down to fit into two compartments – rational resistance and irrational resistance. Rational resistance takes place when a person opposes your presentation or argument on the basis of solid thinking.

A man once said to me that the found it difficult to accept the Christian faith because of its totalitarian concepts. He meant by that the fact that

Christ calls His Church to total commitment and total allegiance. I classified his resistance in discussion as rational resistance, because it stemmed from a rational basis. (Incidentally, it is beyond the scope of this book to focus on the arguments people use when going through what I call rational resistance. Some of these arguments are presented in my book *The Christian Counsellor's Pocket Guide*, published by Kingsway.) My concern in this chapter has been to focus on irrational resistance.

Of course, the most adequate explanation for resistance lies in the Biblical explanation for man's behaviour, which teaches that we possess an inherently perverse nature. 'The heart is deceitful above all things, and desperately wicked' (Jer. 17:9).

Carlyle, the poet and philosopher, said, 'Some people call me a cross-grained and irritable creature, but let me have my own way in everything, and a pleasanter and more agreeable person doesn't exist.'

There is within all of us a perverse nature which insists upon independent self-willed behaviour, and which values such independence above peace of mind and right adjustment with God.

Resistance, in theological terms, is a person's wilful expression of their natural and wilful reluctance to consciously acknowledge the claims of Jesus Christ upon their life. And fundamentally overcoming this resistance requires not just techniques but also the convicting and enlightening work of the Holy Spirit.

10: Watching the expert at work

One of the ways by which we can perfect a technique or an art is by watching an expert at work.

At the age of sixteen I left college to do a five-year apprenticeship in an engineering works. Throughout my first year I did nothing except look over the shoulders of experienced engineers and watch how things were done. Although the theory I had learned in college had given me a good foundation on which to build, it wasn't until I actually saw various tasks being accomplished that it all came together for me.

In this chapter we are going to look over the shoulder, so to speak, of the greatest soulwinner the world has ever seen – the Lord Jesus Christ. We are going to watch Him at work in what is, without doubt, the most wonderful conversion narrative in the Scriptures – the story of the woman at the well.

First, let us set the scene. In the days of Jesus the little village of Sychar was a stopping station between Judea in the south and Galilee in the north. Thousands of years prior to Christ's birth, an Old Testament patriarch by the name of Jacob had dug a well at this strategic intersection lying in the valley between Mount Ebal and Mount Gerazim.

The area in which the well had been dug came to be called Samaria. By the time of Jesus Samaria had become a ghetto for Jews who had intermarried with heathen tribes. Most people who study the Scriptures know that there was a good deal of enmity between the Jews and the Samaritans, but not everybody knows why the enmity existed. It goes back to the year 722 BC when Sargon, the King of Assyria, sacked Samaria and carried away the Ten Tribes into captivity.

Of course, the wholesale deportation of tribes in ancient times was never absolute. Always, when people were deported, a remnant of the population was left to carry on as best they could. When Sargon brought his own people to settle in Samaria, they found a small number of the Israelites still in occupation of the land. After a while some of the remaining Israelites married some of the Assyrians, and their offspring became the people known as Samaritans. Now you can begin to see why it was that the Jews and the Samaritans were so hostile.

The Jews said, 'They are not of the pure stock of Israel.' And the Samaritans said, 'They have tainted us by their bigotry and prejudice.' Matters did not improve, of course, when the Samaritans developed a religion which was closely akin to Judaism. They took the Pentateuch (the first five books of the Bible), and said, 'This is our holy book as well.' Then, because they were excluded from Mount Zion in Jerusalem, they decided to have a holy mount of their own, and so they settled upon Mount Gerazim. Both national and

148

religious sentiment combined to produce in the heart of the Jew a bitter hatred and contempt for his cousin of Samaria.

To a Jew the nastiest word you could use was 'Samaritan'. It meant 'dirty dog'. Among the Samaritans, the term Jew meant someone who was 'snobbish', 'stiff-necked' or 'arrogant'. The gulf between Jews and Samaritans can be seen from the opening remark of the woman at the well, when following Jesus' request for water, she said, 'You are a Jew and I am a Samaritan woman. How can you ask me for a drink? (For Jews do not associate with Samaritans)' (John 4:9, NIV).

Jesus, of course, in His search for the souls of men and women, was prepared to break through all customs and taboos. Many Jews on their way from Jerusalem to Galilee would avoid going through Samaria, taking the longer route which went by way of the Jordan valley. Such, however, was the concern of Christ for the outcasts that He was prepared to cross cultural barriers to meet them.

Someone has said, 'The greatest barriers we have to cross to reach men and women for Christ are not theological but social and cultural.' Our non-Christian friends and neighbours, by their very lifestyle, are poles apart from us. They swear, they drink, they exchange dirty stories, and they haven't the faintest inkling of our evangelical vocabulary. However, a true lover of souls draws near *despite* the obstacles. Evangelism that does not take us into the real world of the unbeliever is not New Testament evangelism.

With these facts as a background, let's now focus in detail on this thrilling encounter of Jesus with the Samaritan woman. All quotations are from the New International Version of the Bible.

Jesus: *Will you give me a drink?*

Comment: Some people are so interested in getting to grips with spiritual issues that other important and relevant matters are ignored or played down. But not Jesus. For Him, at that moment, satisfying His thirst was of primary importance. Jesus was a *natural* witness. His request to the woman was not a device in order to get her attention, but a genuine plea for assistance. He could, of course, have introduced Himself by saying, 'I am Jesus from Nazareth, the son of Mary, but also the Son of God. I am here to talk to you about my Father's Kingdom.' But He didn't. He started at the most natural place – His feeling of thirst. He was being what in today's language is described as authentic. There was no phoniness, no devices, no conversational techniques – just naturalness.

The Samaritan woman: *You are a Jew and I am a Samaritan woman. How can you ask me for a drink? (For Jews do not associate with Samaritans)*

Comment: The woman could have declined to give Jesus a drink, or done so without allowing herself to become involved in a conversation. After all, Jesus was a Jew – a member of the 'stiff-necked' and 'haughty' crowd. Instead she presented an interesting challenge to Jesus. What, I wonder, made her respond in this way? Why did she allow herself to become involved in a conversation with a Jew? The record, of course, tells us nothing about the non-verbal communication of Jesus, but I suspect the woman detected that here was a man of deep honesty and integrity. Everything about Him, I imagine – His tone of voice, the expression on His face, the way He stood, the way He walked – spoke of His dedication to God His Father and His love for the souls of men and women. Did the Samaritan woman pick up this message? I believe she did.

Jesus: If you knew the gift of God and who it is that asks you for a drink, you would have asked him and he would have given you living water.

Comment: Evangelism can be defined as sensitively rubbing one's spiritual finger along the edge of a person's soul, feeling for the areas of obvious need. Somehow in those first few moments Jesus sensed her need – a deep spiritual thirst. Perhaps by an inflection of her voice, facial expression or body language, the Samaritan woman shows that she would be a ready listener to anyone who could meet the deepest need of her heart. Jesus responded to this by introducing Himself, and stating that He was able to meet that spiritual need. The analogy of the water kept the link between the physical and spiritual aspects of the conversation.

The Samaritan woman: Sir, we have nothing to draw with and the well is deep. Where can you get this living water? Are you greater than our father Jacob, who gave us the well and drank

151

from it himself, as did also his sons and his flocks and herds?

Comment: Obviously, Jesus had gained enough of her trust to allow her to discuss the common inheritance they both shared – Jacob's well. Her words have a slight edge of sarcasm, but this could be because of her deep distrust of men. After all, as later information shows, she had been involved in five love affairs. It is not unusual to find in those who distrust people a certain amount of sarcasm. It is a defence which people use when they long to relate to people, but are torn by their desire and their distrust. The fact that she then asked two questions of her own: how can you meet my need?' and, 'Who are you to make this claim?' makes it clear that she was vitally interested. Jesus was leading gently and she was following.

Jesus: Everyone who drinks this water will be thirsty again, but whoever drinks the water I give him will never thirst. Indeed, the water I give him will become in him a spring of water welling up to everlasting life.

Comment: Despite her growing interest and curiosity, Jesus unfolded the message of salvation slowly and gently. His words were carefully chosen so that He didn't go too far ahead of her comprehension and understanding. The mistake many make at this point is that when they see the faintest glimmer of response, they rush right in and expound the entire story of salvation, leaving the person no opportunity to come up for air!

Notice how Jesus, by pressing the analogy of

water, crossed the line between the woman's physical and spiritual needs. He defined living water as something that satisfies the thirst of the soul.

Notice, too, that Jesus didn't duck the woman's questions. He told her that there was a power available to quench her thirst, and that He was the source of that power.

The Samaritan woman: Sir, give me this water so that I won't get thirsty and have to keep coming here to draw water.

Comment: We do not know how long this conversation took up to this point, but it is interesting to observe, now that the woman's scepticism and sarcasm had changed, that she addressed Christ as 'Sir'. Although she could not fully grasp or make the transition from natural water to spiritual water, she openly confessed the dullness of her existence. When a person recognises their need, then they are three-quarters of the way to having it met. Christ had brought her to the place where she was now asking the questions, a sign that she sensed she was on the verge of a great discovery.

Jesus: Go, call your husband and come back.

Comment: Jesus seems to change the subject abruptly here, but the statement is designed to discover whether or not the woman is really willing to face her need. How did Jesus know she had a husband? Was He just 'shooting in the dark'? Or was the woman (as some believe) wearing clothes that marked her out as a woman of loose morals? I believe that this knowledge was conveyed to our

153

Lord by the Holy Spirit. In every evangelistic encounter the Holy Spirit is always present. There is a voice other than yours speaking to that needy soul. Learn to depend on Him, and develop sensitivity to His voice.

What if Jesus had said these words, 'Go, call your husband' in His second sentence to her – what would have happened? Doubtless the conversation would have ended then and there. He timed it so that when it was made, she had developed enough trust in Him to confess her need.

The Samaritan woman: I have no husband.

Comment: As is so often the case when truth is at work, human defence mechanisms come into play. No doubt, the woman had learned from long experience how to parry questions that threatened her security. Defensive actions always reveal insecurity and anxiety, and, in this case, guilt.

Jesus: You are right when you say you have no husband. The fact is, you have had five husbands, and the man you now have is not your husband. What you have just said is quite true.

Comment: How expertly Christ applied the truth to her condition. He did it in a way that brought her face to face with the reality of her life, yet He did not condemn. I know many people who would have been quick to condemn the woman and would have said something like: 'Don't tell me a lie. I know more about you than you think.' We get the mistaken idea that if we do not condemn a certain attitude or action, we will be condoning it. Jesus, of course, could not agree with the woman's lifestyle, but He unveils the truth in such a way that the woman condemns herself. Some would say that Jesus was too sharp in His probing at this point. He certainly seems to be taking a risk. What if she could not have faced this level of truth, wouldn't such a statement cause her to withdraw from Him? No, the Master knew what He was doing. At first it appeared too much for the woman to take, but later she touched upon this very fact to testify that she had found the Christ.

The Samaritan woman: Sir, I can see that you are a prophet. Our fathers worshipped on this mountain, but you Jews claim that the place where we must worship is in Jerusalem.

Comment: The gentle revelation of truth is a little too much for her to bear, so once again she erects a defence. This defence is known to psychologists as 'intellectualisation'. It is an attempt to move someone away from disturbed feelings to the intellectual level, where one feels more able to cope with issues. She was perfectly prepared to debate with Christ the intellectual issue about where God was to be worshipped. Her answer might be paraphrased, 'Oh, I see you are a prophet, let's talk about prophecy.' If she can get Jesus involved in a discussion on the Jew-Samaritan problem, this might help to take the pressure off her disturbed emotions. Had Jesus gone too fast for her? I think not. His incisive statement about her immoral condition had produced great feelings of guilt, so to defend against this, she substituted an intellectual issue for an emotional one.

Jesus: Believe me, woman, a time is coming when you will worship the Father neither on this mountain nor in Jerusalem. You Samaritans worship what you do not know; we worship what we do know, for salvation is from the Jews. Yet a time is coming and has now come when the true worshippers will worship the Father in spirit and truth, for they are the kind of worshippers the Father seeks. God is spirit, and his worshippers must worship in spirit and in truth.

Comment: Jesus, sensing her spiritual pain, accepts the intellectual question and uses it to state an important truth. He could have forced her to face herself more deeply, but that would have been counter-productive. Some Christians withdraw entirely from discussion of intellectual questions, believing them to be 'red herrings', devices of the unconverted to steer the conversation away from the emotions, but this is not always so. John Stott says, 'While we must not pander to a person's intellectual arrogance, we must cater for their intellectual integrity.' After all, the point she was making was an important one. If she followed Jesus, a Jew, then eventually she would have to answer the question of where she worshipped.

Jesus skilfully used the point at issue – where God should be worshipped – to take the woman back into herself. He showed her that the inner life is really the point of communication with God. What was more, Jesus paid the woman a supreme compliment. We might consider Jesus' statement rather profound, but He evidently assumed the woman would be able to draw the parallel between the ancient controversy and the conflict that raged in her own soul.

The Samaritan woman: I know that Messiah (called Christ) is coming. When he comes, he will explain everything to us.

Comment: Jesus' assumption that the woman would comprehend His statement, that the worship of God began in the inner life, is rewarded by her response. She reveals, albeit intellectually, that she is aware that one day a Messiah will come who will bring all conflicts to an end, and enable men and women to live the way God designed them. She also reveals by this statement that she is on the point of giving up her intellectual defence, and appears to show some concern about the coming of the Messiah. Was she putting out a feeler that the one standing before her might be the Christ? Did she wonder that this stranger might be the Anointed One, yet hardly dare express it? Certainly she recognises that if her disordered life is to be put right then she needs supernatural aid.

Jesus: I who speak to you am he.

Comment: As we saw earlier, despite the woman's obvious curiosity and interest, Jesus did not reveal the whole story at once. The more interested she became, the more He revealed. Then when her curiosity had reached its highest point, He identified

Himself as the Christ. Some Bible commentators say that Jesus revealed Himself more openly to this Samaritan woman than He did to His own disciples. Why was this so? In my view, her total openness and honesty had brought her to a place where it was easy for Christ to reveal Himself to her. With others, even the disciples, Jesus had to hold back some things so that He would not be exploited by those with mixed motives or partial insight. The Samaritan woman, though a deep-dyed sinner, was so open to His approach that He was able to reveal Himself fully to her. Perhaps this is what Jesus had in mind when He said to the chief priests and elders: 'The tax collectors and the prostitutes are entering the kingdom of God ahead of you' (Matt. 21:31 NIV).

In declaring that He was the Messiah, our Lord reached the crucial point of the Gospel. Similarly, when we are involved in conversations about Christ, it is our duty to bring a non-Christian face to face with the fact that they have to decide *for* or *against* Him. Jesus brought the Samaritan woman to the point of decision. And He did it in such a way that did not damage her rights as a person. He did not force her to make a decision, but conducted the conversation in such a way that made her decide whether she would reject her new-found insight and sink deeper into sin or commit herself to Christ and be made whole.

Conclusion: When Christ's disciples returned to the scene, after having gone into the village to buy meat, we read that they were surprised to find him talking to a woman. Not only did Christ speak to a Samaritan woman – a cultural taboo – but He taught her truths concerning God although the Rabbinical law stated that the Scriptures should not be taught privately to a woman. No wonder, as one translator puts it, the disciples, when they returned, were shocked to find him talking to a woman.

While the disciples were talking to Jesus, the Samaritan woman ran to the nearby village and announced to everyone who would listen, 'Come, see a man who told me everything I ever did. Could this be the Christ?'

Her announcement of the Messiah was framed in the form of a question, but I think we can take it as her confession of faith. Nothing more is said in the Scriptures about this woman except that the inhabitants of the village of Sychar rushed out to meet Jesus and invited Him into their village as an honoured guest. During His two-day stay with them, we read that 'because of his words many more became believers' (John 4:41, NIV).

And what is perhaps one of the most significant comments in the whole of the Gospels comes right at the end of the story:

'They said to the woman, "We no longer believe just because of what you said; now we have heard for ourselves, and we know that this man really is the Saviour of the world" ' (John 4:42, NIV).

What have we learned by looking over the shoulder of Jesus as He so skilfully led the Samaritan woman into an awareness of who He was and the purpose of His mission on the earth?

Is it not this? If we are to follow in our Master's footsteps and win people to Him, then we must:

* be willing to cross cultural boundaries and barriers to reach them
* accept them as they are
* allow them to confess their own personal need
* respect their individuality
* point the way to release from guilt
* use the truth to challenge them
* introduce them to the Master

Otherwise we will never get beyond asking parched souls for a drink of water.

11: How to lead a person to Christ

Happily, sharing one's faith with others will result at times in the person being willing and ready to commit themselves to Jesus Christ. This does not mean, of course, that every time we witness we must expect such a decision. That would be unrealistic, to say the least. But we do need to be alert and sensitive to what is going on in a person's heart, so that we can help them make that great and momentous decision.

When it appears right and appropriate to do so, we ought never to shrink from asking a person to make a decision for Jesus Christ. Many Christians, I have discovered, have great difficulty with this issue. They can give a 'good reason for the hope that is within them' or share their personal testimony with radiant enthusiasm, but when it comes to asking a person to commit themselves to the Saviour, they feel somewhat lost and inadequate.

I remember discussing this many years ago with a man who told me that although he was deeply involved in the work of personal evangelism, he had never actually led a person to Christ. He said to me, 'I can lead a person to the Living Water, but I am unable to ask them to drink?' Is this your problem?

When you think about it, it is quite tragic that a moment comes in witnessing when the person is willing – or almost willing – but the direct question isn't put. Times without number, tremulous souls have as much as admitted that they would have surrendered to Christ years ago if they had been asked. I tremble at the thought of how many I have failed in this way.

The importance of a decision

A personal decision to commit one's life to Jesus Christ is the most important issue to be settled. But decision is not conversion, of course, as many theologians have been at pains to point out. Decision is an act of the human will; conversion is an act of God.

Decision is not to be despised because of that, as conversion cannot take place until a person agrees, by an act of will, to admit Jesus Christ into their life. What a premium God places upon the human will. The great God and Creator of the universe deigns to condescend to knock at the door of a person's heart, and will not enter their lives unless accepted and admitted.

There are some Christians, of course, who cannot ever remember making a definite decision to receive Christ. Brought up, perhaps, in a Christian home where Christ was present in all His power they quietly and gradually embraced the faith without being conscious of a particular moment when that happened.

Are they any less Christian because they cannot

point to a definite moment of conversion? Of course not! After all a birth certificate is not the best evidence that one is alive.

I believe, however, that although a person may not be able to identify a precise moment of decision and conversion, yet such a moment definitely exists.

When I study the Scriptures, I see quite clearly that a person *must* pass from death into life, *must* experience a transformation if they are to enter the Kingdom of God and *must* at some point cross that mysterious line that separates a sinner from the Saviour. Although some may not remember the precise moment of conversion, I believe it to be theologically correct to say that somewhere, sometime, that person reached out in faith to Jesus Christ and was saved. The fact that no such event can be brought to mind is unimportant, in my view, providing that person knows the full assurance of salvation and has no doubts about their personal relationship with Jesus Christ.

In an age like the present, where Christian influence in the home is not perhaps as strong as it was in the early part of this century, it seems that Christians who have come into the church in the past couple of decades are those who can remember a clear moment of decision. It is my belief that the changing pattern of the times will produce in the future more Christians who pass through a crisis period or a precise moment of conversion. That is why we need to spend a few minutes discussing the ramifications of personal decision for Christ.

Some people have a growing awareness of Christ or a deepening awareness of spiritual matters, but in order for the issues to be clarified they must be brought to a definite commitment. A conscious commitment to Christ has great spiritual and psychological value. It helps to validate one's experience and pinpoint issues, so that when, at some later date, Satan might tempt one over the issue of lack of assurance, one can say, 'This is where it happened. I received Christ and the matter was settled once and for all.'

Thirty-two years ago, I committed my life and my love to Enid, who is my wife. I did not accept her as an interesting person with whom I could while away a few hours now and again. I fell deeply in love with her. She fully occupied my thoughts, and became more important to me than any other human being. I decided that I did not want to live apart from her, and as she felt the same way about me, we committed our lives to each other. That commitment took place at a certain time in a certain place – a small church in the little town of Helston, Cornwall.

I cannot for the life of me remember the exact moment when I fell in love with Enid. But I can remember with amazing clarity the moment that I committed myself to her with the words: 'I will.' That commitment meant so much to me that although there have been times when our marriage has been very insecure and fraught with problems, I have never once considered breaking that commitment. It has, in my opinion, helped to cement us together in a way that nothing else could have done.

I have little doubt that the best way a person can come into the kingdom of God is by making a conscious and deliberate commitment to Christ.

But I also accept that some people, for the reasons I have given, may have made such a decision unconsciously.

One thing is clear: it is a marvellous and wonderful privilege to get people to lay themselves open to Jesus Christ, to invite Him in, to ask His help, to dedicate their entire life to the Son of God.

Asking for the decision

Let's assume that having shared your faith with someone in the way suggested in this book, you sense that the person to whom you have been witnessing is close to the point of decision. How then do you go about the task of asking for a decision and actually leading the person to Christ?

1. Begin by summarising the basic content of the Gospel

The question is often debated in evangelical circles: what is the minimum of truth a person needs to know in order to become a Christian? There is no easy answer to that question. The Bible doesn't give us an irreducible minimum although there are Christians who argue that it does.

I personally believe, however, that there are five essentials which must be presented to a person who is about to become a Christian. These essentials were used by the leaders of the great eighteenth century evangelical revival and they held that the New Testament supported and sustained these beliefs. They are as follows:

1. Everyone needs eternal life
2. Everyone may have eternal life
3. Everyone who receives it knows that they have it
4. Everyone must witness to its possession
5. Everyone must allow the life of God within them to deepen and develop

When I am involved in leading a person to Christ, I go over these five basic truths in the simplest language.

Everyone needs eternal life. The life we have when we are born is a life that is tainted by sin and stained by impurity. Because of that, no one, for all their talk of experiencing life, has ever really had it. In the profoundest sense possible to human beings they have never been born.

Everyone may have eternal life. Such is the matchless grace of God that whoever reaches out, though their conscience condemn, the offer is for *them*. The most stubborn and resistant sinner may have eternal life. The way to receive it is by acknowledging one is a sinner, and by repenting and believing the Gospel.

I make a point of stressing the importance of repentance because I believe that the more clearly a person understands repentance, the more meaningful his conversion. But in order to define repentance, one must first define sin. What is sin?

Sin is basically self-centredness. It is pushing God out of the centre of one's life, and allowing the ego to take over the part that God designed for Himself. Some people define sin as adultery, lying, stealing, cheating, and so on. Those are *sins*. Sin is man shaking his fist in God's face and saying, 'I want to run my life on my own terms.' And it is this which must be repented of.

I define repentance, therefore, as telling God one is sorry for having displaced Him from one's life, and that now He is to be allowed in to one's life to rule and reign as one's rightful Lord.

Let me repeat this statement, for I believe it to be of the utmost importance. *The more clearly sin and repentance are defined, the more clearly does a person come to faith in Christ.* Unless the ego is firmly renounced in the act of conversion, then it will raise its head, time and time again, to challenge that person in their ongoing Christian life.

Everyone who receives it knows that they have it. To have the life of God pulsing in one's soul, and not know it, is impossible. John Wesley believed that some people were saved and yet had no assurance of it. But for anyone to receive Christ, and not know it, is strange and abnormal.

I explain at this point that when Christ is admitted into one's life, He brings an inward witness and a supply of moral power that makes itself felt in the inner recesses of the soul. One should not live, of course, on fluctuating feeling, but one can expect to know that quiet conscious flow of power that arises from the indwelling Christ.

Everyone must witness to its possession. No one must carry eternal life around in their soul as if it were a guilty secret. It is not to be hugged to oneself and treated as if it were a private personal possession. Nothing is really ours until we share it. All expression deepens impression. It is a law of the personality that that which is not expressed dies. If there is no outflow, the inflow automatically stops.

There are two seas in Palestine. One is the fresh and fruitful Sea of Galilee. The other, the Dead Sea, bitter and barren. Why the difference? Galilee both takes and gives. The Dead Sea has no outlet.

When Peter spoke to the man at the Beautiful Gate in the book of Acts, he made a statement that shows that to have is not enough. 'Such as I have,' said Peter, 'I give' (Acts 3:1–11). The possession of eternal life becomes a debt. I do not own it; I *owe* it.

Everyone must allow the life of God within them to deepen and develop. The life of God, like all life, involves growth. No limit must be put on its development. Whatever decay mars the life of men, no decay mars the life of God.

John Wesley impressed upon his converts as soon as they came to Christ, that something had *begun*. 'New life has come into your heart in the person of the Holy Spirit,' he would say. 'It is the life of God – in *you*. Let Him rule. Let Him reign. Put no limit on what He can do in your life. And go on growing.'

These five basic essentials provide, so I believe, a sound framework within which to introduce a person to Christ; and they are as true for Christ's ambassadors in this century as they were for the heralds of God in the eighteenth century. They enable an ambassador of Christ to acquaint an enquirer with the basic facts of the Gospel. When understood, they enable him to stand fast in the truth of God.

Now I realise, of course, that the five principles with which I feel comfortable may not suit you. It may be that you find yourself more at home with the Four Spiritual Laws, or some other kind of presentation. But whatever method you use, explain it in simple language and in the clearest possible terms.

After you have summarised the basic content of the Gospel, thus enabling the person to comprehend God's wonderful plan of salvation – what then?

2. Clarify what it is you are asking the person to do.

Explain that the way by which Christ comes into a person's life is by invitation only. That means the person has to open their life to Christ in an act of commitment. This is best achieved by verbally asking Christ to come in. At this stage, say something like this: 'Now, in order for Christ to enter your life, you will need to open your life to Him by inviting Him in. This means that in a moment we are going to pray together. Now I realise that you may never have prayed or spoken to God before in your life, so let me just share with you what is involved.'

Go on then to explain (again in simple language) what prayer is all about. Prayer is communication with God. It is the way in which a human being makes contact with the creator of the universe. Prayer is conversation, talking to

169

God in the same way that we talk to everyone else.

I love the story told by Howard Hendricks of the young man who had attended several home Bible studies and eventually decided he wanted to accept Christ. When Howard invited him to pray, he said, 'Howard, I have a problem. I can't pray like you and the other fellows.'

'That's no problem,' Howard assured him. 'Thank God you don't pray like us!'

He didn't quite understand that statement, but anyway he bowed his head. This is what he said:

'Lord, this is Jim. I'm the one You met last Thursday night over at . . . I hope you'll forgive me 'cause I can't say it the way these guys can. Maybe when I know You as long as they do, I'll do a better job, but I'd like You to know I love You from the bottom of my heart, and I want You in my life. Thank You, Lord. Amen.'

Howard Hendricks says that was one of the most moving prayers he had ever heard in his life; and I can believe it.

Don't worry too much if your convert is unable to pray. Tell him that prayer is talking to God in ordinary language – nothing put on, no airs and graces – just natural conversation.

Ask if they would like you to pray first. Explain that if they find it difficult to pray, then you will be prepared to help by supplying the words. But don't do this unless it is absolutely necessary. There is something very important happening to a person who stumbles and fumbles for words when praying. If you can resist rushing in to help, you may find that the prayer they utter, though perhaps inarticulate and almost unintelligible, may be the beginnings of a great spiritual experience for them as, through their own words, they make contact with the living God.

Whatever you do, don't make the commitment for them. You can witness, pray, persuade, but the commitment to Christ, and the prayer of dedication, must be their own. The act of commitment has a psychological benefit as well as a spiritual one. They will be able, in the future, to point to a specific time and place, and recall what happened, thus helping to maintain their confidence.

The prayer should contain what they want to put into it.

When the person to whom you have witnessed has made their commitment, spend some time sharing with them. Make arrangements to give them every encouragement and support you can.

After people have committed themselves to Christ, their responses might differ. Some have a great sense of joy; others weep. Some may not feel anything in particular, just a quiet conviction that they have done what they know they should.

After a little while, and before leaving them, get them to give their first Christian testimony, by asking them something like this: what has taken place in your life in the last hour? This will reinforce what has happened, for, as we said earlier, all expression deepens impression.

I pray with all my heart that if you have not known it before, you will experience the joy in the not too distant future of not only witnessing for your Lord but of actually leading someone to Jesus Christ.

3. Explain the basic principles of how to grow 'in Christ'

One of the major concerns in the field of evangelism is the high mortality rate amongst those who claim to be born again. It is higher in some areas of evangelism (such as mass crusades) than in others. But all who are involved in leading men and women to Jesus Christ are intensely concerned about those who fall away. Not a few begin only to perish in infancy.

Some explain this high mortality rate by referring to the parable of the sower and the seed. 'Our Lord,' they say, 'had a similar experience. Some seed fell by the wayside, some fell where there was no depth of earth and some where the thorns grew up and choked it. We cannot expect to have different results from His.'

Allowing for the fact that a certain percentage of those who make a decision for Jesus Christ 'fall by the wayside', there is, I believe, a good deal we can do to ensure that our converts maintain their spiritual enthusiasm as they begin 'the steep ascent to heaven'.

What steps should we take to encourage new converts to 'press on to perfection'? What can we do to help those begotten by the Holy Spirit move toward maturity?

Firstly, *we ought to encourage them to join a Bible believing church or fellowship*. Some evangelists state quite openly that the church is often to blame for the mortality amongst young believers. 'If the church were warm and welcoming

172

and spiritually alive, these young Christians would not die,' they say.

Samuel Chadwick, one time principal of Cliff College, blamed himself on one occasion for sending a new convert to a church which was cold and dead. He said, 'It was like putting a baby in the arms of a corpse.'

Fortunately, there are signs everywhere that churches and fellowships are more alive and alert to the needs of new converts than they have been for a number of decades.

Just recently I talked to a young man who told me that he had been a Christian for just over a year. 'Wonderful,' I said, 'the first year of Christian experience is one of the most exciting periods of one's life. It gets better as one goes on, but there is something very special about one's first full year as a Christian.'

'Well,' he replied, 'it's been rather touch and go to be quite honest with you. All my life I have been a healthy individual, but for some reason the past twelve months have been filled with sickness and at times agonizing pain. But the other day someone let something slip in my church that moved me to the depth of my being. I found out that for close on a year thirty members had covenanted to pray for me and my family in a round-the-clock prayer chain, which went on uninterrupted until just a few weeks ago. Miraculously my health recovered, and the doctor said there was no explanation for my return to health apart from what he described as 'spiritual and not medical reasons'.

What a joy it was to that young Christian to know that he was surrounded by people who would pray for him when he was engulfed and overwhelmed by personal problems.

Secondly, *we ought to encourage new converts to have a daily quiet time with God*. There is no way we can grow in the Christian life when we belittle, ignore or skip regular times of secret communion with God. The saints down the ages have been of one mind in this. Prayer, Bible reading and listening to God are the key words. Those who go around searching for a new 'secret' of spiritual growth are really quite foolish. If there is a *new* secret, how can we explain the health and growth of the saints of old?

Prayer, Bible reading and listening to God – what words they are to those who truly love the Lord!

Prayer! The way to know Christ with intimacy is to talk to Him, to talk to Him often and to talk for more than just a few moments. New Christians, however, need a pattern or a plan for praying. Nothing complicated or too restricting, but something plain and simple. The pattern I usually give to new converts is this. I take the acrostic:

P – Praise
R – Reflect
A – Ask
Y – Yearn

It is always good to begin one's private communication with God in *Praise*. And there is so much to praise Him for. One needs only to think of the wonder of being pardoned and forgiven.

174

Pardon – from an offended God!
  Pardon – for sins of deepest dye!
Pardon – bestowed through Jesus' blood!
  Pardon – that brings the rebel nigh!
Who is a pardoning God like Thee?
  Or who has grace so rich and free?

R stands for Reflect. It's simply amazing what happens to one's heart when one reflects on the goodness and mercy of God. Even in rare days of extreme difficulties, there is always something to be thankful for. The mind, when put to work, can soon come up with reasons for rejoicing. Health, home, friends, the privilege of prayer . . . . When we reflect on such things, it is not long before the heart swells with gratitude and one's mood is set for the day that lies ahead.

A stands for Ask. It is always right to ask God for the things we need in life. Jesus encouraged us to do so. 'Ask,' He said, 'and it will be given to you; seek and you will find; knock and the door will be opened to you' (Matt. 7:7, NIV).

It is right also to ask on behalf of others. When we ask for ourselves, we call our prayer petition. When we ask on behalf of others, that is known as *intercession.* How comforting to know that when we speak, God listens. So pour it out. His ear is ever open to His needy children's cry.

Y stand for Yearn. To 'yearn' is to desire something with longing and passion. Every time we come into God's presence, our greatest longing should be to become more and more like Jesus.

What would happen if every Christian *yearned* to be more like Him? I will tell you. The yearning would move us more and more in His direction until we found that our thoughts were to be like His thoughts, our wills like His will, our love like His love and our lives like His life. It would be as if Christ were thinking in us, willing in us, loving in us and living out His radiant life in every area of our personality.

'Blessed are those who hunger and thirst for righteousness,' said Jesus in His Sermon on the Mount (Matt. 5:6, NIV). And why are they 'blessed'. The answer is this: 'they will be filled' or *satisfied*. The greater our yearning for Him, the more He is able to pour into us.

Prayer of course, is conversation. And like all conversation, it has two sides to it – talking and listening. Listening to God is something that many who have been on the Christian way for some time still regard as a mystery. They think it is a metaphor. They have never learned to disentangle the voice of God from the voices that flow out of the subconscious. So let us teach new Christians how to listen to God, to wait before Him for minutes, and learn by experience to recognise His voice. It doesn't come easily. But then neither does learning the piano, or any other musical instrument. Listening to God is an art. And like all art forms, practice makes perfect.

Thirdly, *we ought to encourage new converts to read the Bible regularly – daily if possible*. I believe that the wisest advice ever given to me when I was a young Christian was to fence off a certain part of each day and use it to read the Bible and pray. The discipline this produced in me has helped me in many of life's battles.

New Christians, of course, need more direction than just having a Bible stuck under their nose

176

and being told: 'Here's Genesis, begin there and read it all the way through to the end.'

I like to suggest to them that they begin with John's Gospel, and quietly work their way through that, and then read the other Gospels so that they form a composite picture of what Christ was like and who He really is. Later, they can be introduced to the epistles and then parts of the Old Testament, such as the book of Psalms. It ought to go without saying that a modern translation, such as the New International Version or the Good News Bible is helpful.

We ought to explain to new Christians that the Bible is a unique volume. Whatever degree of inspiration may be attached to other writings, this one is the only book on earth that contains the record of God's incarnate Son, the spiritual pilgrimage of the race among whom Christ was born, and the birth and growth of the Christian Church. The Bible is no ordinary book. A volume that was so miraculously brought together requires divine help to be understood. This is why every time we open its pages we ought to pray for receptiveness of mind.

It ought also to be impressed upon all new converts that not only did God speak through the Bible to men and women in the past, but that *He speaks through it still*. It is a living word. Encourage them to study it daily, and memorise passages of it. The main purpose of the Bible is to bring the mind of Christ into *our* minds. To imagine that it is possible to gain the mind of Christ without spending time in the Bible is folly of the highest order.

Fourthly, *we ought to encourage new converts*

177

to share their faith with others. You will remember that in the previous chapter we looked at Jesus in His encounter with the woman at the well. That conversation resulted in the woman leaving her water pot and going into the city to say, 'Come, see a man who told me everything I ever did.'

The outcome of that conversation was a witness. 'You haven't got them in,' said a famous evangelist, 'until you get them out.' The instinct to share Christ is present in the heart of every Christian – it needs discipline and direction, however, to bring it out.

Rags, an airedale, missing three days, was found when a faint barking was heard from a fifty-foot dry well. A man was lowered into the well and Rags was brought up, uninjured, but weak from lack of food.

The dog quickly consumed some food and water that was given to him, and then, when the group who had gathered at the top of the well to witness the rescue, tried to take Rags home, he kept running to the top of the well, looking down, and barking for all he was worth.

Eventually one of the group descended into the well to discover the cause of Rag's concern. He found a rabbit, frightened, hungry and extremely timid. When the rabbit was brought up safely, Rags sniffed him and then willingly headed for home.

The same impulse is in the heart of every person who has experienced the saving power of Jesus Christ – he cannot be content to be rescued alone. He can be content only when those who have shared his pit have been saved.

A missionary evangelist claims that just as a

new Christian must be faced with the need to discipline himself in relation to prayer, the reading of the Scriptures and linking himself to a live church, so must he discipline himself to the task of sharing with others the fact of his conversion. 'You can't always rely on the instinct to share,' he says. 'It is there, but like all other instincts, it needs the strength of discipline to effectively bring it out.'

Many new Christians fail here. They become disciplined in prayer and reading the Word, but they never discipline themselves to share. If a happening or a conversation jolts it out of them, well and good. But sharing seems to depend on accident more than choice – the result of a whim rather than the will.

So encourage every person you lead to Christ to discipline himself to sharing with others, at appropriate times, the testimony of his conversion to Jesus Christ.

For, as Dr Billy Graham says, 'Evangelism is not complete until the evangelised become evangelists.'

12: 'So send I you'

Professor Chad Walsh in his book *Early Christians of the Twenty-first Century*, says, 'I suspect that Satan has called off his attempt to convert people to agnosticism. After all, if a man travels far enough away from Christianity, he is likely to see it in its proper perspective and decide that it is true. It is much safer from Satan's point of view to vaccinate a man with a mild case of Christianity so as to protect him from the real disease.'

You have only to examine the Acts of the Apostles to see that most of the people featured in its pages were men and women who had caught the 'real disease'. They were so gripped and possessed with the truth and reality of the Gospel that they said on one occasion: 'We cannot stop telling about the wonderful things we saw Jesus do and heard him say' (Acts 4:20, TLB).

What a beautiful description of witnessing – 'We cannot stop telling about the wonderful . . . Jesus.'

Well, just as Jesus had His witnesses in that first century, so are they present in this century too. Let me introduce you, in this final chapter, to some of the people I have met in my travels who have struck me as being outstanding witnesses for Jesus Christ. They are not preachers or ordained ministers, but ordinary men and women who have become infected with the 'real disease' of Christianity and have made it communicable.

Bryn – thrown in at the deep end

Bryn, a trainee teacher and a member of my church in a small town near Swansea, South Wales, said to me one Sunday evening, 'I'm losing my faith. The Gospel doesn't seem to excite me as it once did. Can you help me put my finger on the problem?'

We talked for a while and I realised that Bryn was losing confidence in the power of the Gospel, because, for some time, he hadn't seen it explode in another person's life.

'Join me next Saturday,' I said, 'and we'll go on a door-to-door campaign, and share Christ with as many people as we can.'

He agreed, and so the next Saturday morning both of us set out together to share our faith with people in a certain street.

After I had spoken to a number of housewives who had opened their doors to us, I said, 'The next house is yours.' He almost fainted. When we came to the next one, I fully expected to see him hesitate and fumble, and I prepared myself to rescue him if the worst came to the worst. Bryn, however, poured out his soul in such a way that the young couple who answered the door invited us in and received Christ right there in their own front room.

From that moment, Bryn was a new man. He became so transformed that within weeks he had gathered around him a group of young people whom he trained in the art of house-to-house visitation. This group of young people went systematically from house to house until the whole town was covered. Dozens of people were won to Christ, some of whom joined the church and became, in turn, radiant witnesses to the Gospel themselves.

Bjorn and a remarkable telephone call

Bjorn, a young Swedish medical doctor, took me to his home for some light refreshments, following a service at which I had preached in the town of Gottenburg, Sweden. My subject that night had been 'Sharing the Faith', and I had tried to encourage the people present to share their faith with their friends and neighbours, and invite them to the special services I was holding in the town.

Bjorn had also invited a group of young people to his home and as we all sat around the supper table, he said, 'Your message has fired me with such a desire to share Jesus Christ with someone that I don't think I can go to sleep tonight without telling someone about Him.'

Just then one of the young people broke in and said, 'Why don't we telephone someone – anyone – and sing to them about the love of Jesus?'

They all thought it was a good idea, so someone picked up a telephone directory, selected a name and a number, and proceeded to dial it. As soon as the telephone was picked up at the other end, they got around the mouthpiece and sang the song:

> *'Jesus is the Answer, to the world today*
> *Without Him there's no living,*
> *Without Him there's no Way.'*

When they had finished singing, they paused to hear what kind of reaction it had brought. After a few moments of silence, they heard some heavy sobbing and a voice said, 'You will never know what those words have meant to me. This very moment I was just about to end my life . . . please tell me if Jesus can help me solve my problems?'

Within minutes Bjorn and the young people made their way to the person's house, and led her to joyous acceptance of the Lord Jesus Christ.

Jean and 'Chariots of Fire'

Jean, a twenty-eight-year-old schoolteacher, teaches English at a school in Middlesex. She told me that she had many opportunities to witness for Christ in her school, and as long as she uses good judgment, she doesn't get into any difficulties over it.

One day she announced to her class that she had purchased some tickets for the film 'Chariots of Fire', and whoever would agree to submitting a report on the film could have them – gratis. Five girls accepted the offer, and after seeing the film and submitting their reports, they asked if they could meet privately with Jean to discuss the 'spiritual implications of the film'.

Jean invited them to her home, and shared with them the basic truths of the Gospel. Two of the girls said that they would like to receive Christ for themselves, and there and then made a commitment to the Lord Jesus Christ.

I am convinced that if we are really serious about sharing Christ with others, and witnessing to our faith, then God drops ideas in our minds as how best to do it. And any action we take must, of course, be tempered by a genuine concern for the person we are trying to win – not just gaining a spiritual scalp!

Bill and his unique approach

Bill, a mechanic I knew, worked in a garage in Colchester. Every time I dropped in I found him sharing Christ in such an uninhibited manner that I invited him to share with a group of Christians in my church the methods he adopted in his day-to-day witnessing.

He told the group, 'Whenever a customer walks in, I ask the Lord if He wants me to say anything to this person of a spiritual nature. I believe that timing is most important. If a person seems to be in a hurry, then, however strongly I feel, I usually let it pass. But when God impresses me to speak to someone, I relate the Gospel to their most obvious interest of the present moment – their car.

I usually say, 'Your car is ready, sir. Just be careful how you look after it, for a car is like the human body, it has to be kept in good order if it is to function properly. And it takes the right kind of driver to go where he wants to go – and go safely.' I then hand over a fair bill for the work and, usually, an appropriate Gospel tract.'

After Bill had shared with the group the basis

of his approach to people, I asked if there was anyone who might like to ask Bill some questions concerning his style of witnessing.

One man rose to his feet and said, 'Well, I haven't got a question, but I would like to say that I have been on the receiving end of Bill's evangelism, and although he doesn't know it, the way he spoke to me, and the concern he showed for my spiritual welfare, was used by the Lord to bring me to Himself. It was a long struggle, but the words Bill said to me one day while I was in his garage were used by the Holy Spirit to bring me to Christ.'

During the time I was in Colchester, I learned that Bill had been influential in helping dozens of people make a decision for Jesus Christ. Although up to the time I knew him, he had never actually led anyone to Christ, he had been used time and time again by the Lord in opening up a person's mind to the importance of a Christian commitment.

When I asked Bill how he felt about the fact that he had never actually led a person to Christ, he said, 'That to me is not the important thing. If the occasion arises I will be ready for it, but the way I see it, my role as a Christian is not to force a person to make a decision, but simply to give myself to God as an instrument for His use.'

Marion's new strategy

Marion, a young wife I knew in the Midlands, had a non-Christian husband whom she desperately tried to win to the Lord Jesus Christ. But as so often happens, she tried to ram the Gospel down

185

his throat. She played Gospel records to him incessantly, put religious tracts in his lunch box, and used every opportunity she could to present him with the facts of the Gospel.

One day when he arrived home, he found his wife had prepared for him a deliciously cooked meal of steak and potatoes. As he sat down to eat, she said, 'What's that on your plate?'

The husband looked nonplussed for a moment, then said, 'It's steak, isn't it?'

'Yes, it's steak,' said his wife. 'And where does steak come from?'

'From cows.'

'And who made cows?'

'God.'

'That's right!' – and then launching into a prepared evangelistic spiel, she presented to him ten reasons why he should put God first in his life.

One day, following a seminar I conducted in the Midlands on the subject of *Successful Family Living* she came to me and asked for my opinion on why she had failed to win her husband to Christ.

I referred her to 1 Peter 3:1–2, where Paul says, 'Wives, fit in with your husbands' plans; for then if they refuse to listen when you talk to them about the Lord, they will be won by your respectful, pure behaviour. Your godly lives will speak to them better than any words' (TLB).

'Your task is not to convert your husband,' I said, 'but to love him. Stop preaching, show him respect, and show as much concern for him as a person as you do for his soul.'

She took my advice. Yes, you've guessed it!

One day he, too, accepted Christ into his life as Saviour and Lord.

Dave and the St John Ambulance Brigade

I have a friend named Dave whom some people would regard as a low-key witness. He doesn't say a great deal, but his concern for people and his ability to make friends has been greatly used by the Holy Spirit in leading dozens of people to Christ.

On one occasion when I visited him I found him attired in a St John Ambulance Brigade uniform. 'I didn't know you were a St John Ambulance man,' I said.

'Well, it's like this,' he drawled, and then told me a story that moved me almost to tears.

Dave had taken an interest in a young boy who was a product of a broken home. The boy, now being fostered by a neighbour, had remarked to Dave that he was interested in becoming a member of the St John Ambulance Brigade. 'We'll join together,' said Dave. 'I'm in my fifties but one is never too old to learn.'

Dave and his young friend Don attended classes together, and afterwards they would both go home to Dave's house and talk about what they had learned that night in the class. Occasionally talk would shift from shoulder-slings and sprained ankles to matters relating to the Christian faith.

One night after a particularly interesting discussion on spiritual matters, Don said he would give anything in the world to have the same kind of peace that Dave seemed to possess. 'It's yours for the asking,' said Dave.

Together they knelt on the carpet, and Don crossed the line of decision and surrendered his heart and life to Christ. Today Don is a missionary in the Far East and has won countless souls to the Kingdom of God.

We might not be preachers or public speakers, but we can all find ways of showing love and concern – at home, at work, at school or in the neighbourhood.

The Davies sisters

In Sheffield, three sisters, the Davies sisters, made a commitment one night to reach out to everyone they could with the message of God's great love and concern. They didn't know where to start, but they kept on saying in their daily prayers, 'Lord, we're available.'

Then it happened!

One night a neighbour knocked on the door and said, 'Please forgive me for disturbing you, but I've watched you going to church regularly, and as my wife has just walked out on me, leaving me with three young children, I wondered if there was anything you could do to help me?'

The Davies sisters were down the road like a shot. They had the children prepared for bed in a matter of minutes, and they sat up until 2 am in the morning working out a schedule of help and assistance for the unfortunate husband.

Soon the news of the way they were helping spread throughout the whole neighbourhood, and within weeks their home became a rescue station for people who were facing emergencies. The people of the neighbourhood learned that here

188

were three women who cared, and, as a result, the phone rings day and night with people who are desperate for help or a word of encouragement.

One of the sisters told me in a recent letter that one in ten people they help make a commitment to Jesus Christ. And they help on average three hundred people a year!

Just as God was in charge of the situation when the Davies sisters said, 'Lord, we're available,' so you can be sure that He'll be in charge of your endeavours to communicate His love.

As one preacher puts it. 'Be content to be the instrument, and let Him determine how long it takes to strike gold.'

If we are alert and ready, the Lord will send countless opportunities our way to share His love with the people we meet. And if we are on His wavelength, He will give us the spiritual discernment to be able to say and do the right thing for Him.

These true experiences of born-again Christians, who witness for Christ in their daily lives, are a direct fulfilment of the words of Jesus: 'As my Father hath sent me, even so send I you' (John 20:21). The Father sent the Son into the world to live, to work, and to show others the way to Him. As Christ's followers, we must let Him continue the work through us.

This does not mean, as we have seen, that we must constantly buttonhole people about their relationship to God. Witnessing should be natural – an integral part of our character and personality. And that also means that how we live must match what we say or else no one will listen to our message.

Few of us will be called to be preachers, or missionaries, but God has called each one of us to share our faith among the circle of our friends, family and acquaintances.

And what if we don't?

Then, quite simply, the Gospel will not be made known.

There is a legend which recounts the return of Jesus Christ to heaven following His successful mission on earth. The angel Gabriel looked upon the marks of the nail prints in Christ's hands and feet and said, 'Master, how terribly you must have suffered down there on that cruel cross.'

'Yes,' said the Master, 'I did – but there was just no other way the world could be saved. It was worth all the pain.'

Gabriel then asked, 'Master, does everyone know just how much you loved them, and what it cost you to pay the price for their sin?'

'Oh no, not yet. At this moment only a mere handful of people know.'

'What steps have you taken to tell everyone the story of your love for them?'

'I have asked my disciples Peter, James, John and the others to tell as many as they can the story of my love. Those who receive it will then tell others and so on until the whole of mankind will have heard about me and why I died upon the Cross.'

Gabriel frowned and looked sceptical. 'But Master, what if Peter, James or John and the others who are your followers grow tired of the task? What if for some reason they become disinclined to make the message known? Or what will happen if later down the centuries people stop telling the Good News for one reason or another? Have you made any other plans?'

Jesus looked at Gabriel with great understanding and simply said, 'No, I have no other plan.'